LIPSMACKIN'
CAST IRON COOKIN'

LIPSMACKIN' CAST IRON COOKIN'

Easy and Delicious Cast Iron Recipes for Camping

CHRISTINE AND TIM CONNERS

ESSEX, CONNECTICUT

FALCONGUIDES®

An imprint of Globe Pequot, the trade division of
The Rowman & Littlefield Publishing Group, Inc.
4501 Forbes Blvd., Ste. 200
Lanham, MD 20706
www.rowman.com

Falcon and FalconGuides are registered trademarks and Make Adventure Your Story is a
trademark of The Rowman & Littlefield Publishing Group, Inc.

Distributed by NATIONAL BOOK NETWORK

British Library Cataloguing in Publication Information available

Library of Congress Cataloging-in-Publication Data

Names: Conners, Christine, author. | Conners, Tim, author.
Title: Lipsmackin' cast iron cookin' : easy and delicious cast iron recipes
  for camping / Christine and Tim Conners.
Other titles: Lipsmacking cast iron cooking
Description: Essex, Connecticut : Falcon Guides, [2023] | Includes index.
Identifiers: LCCN 2022046976 (print) | LCCN 2022046977 (ebook) | ISBN
  9781493067213 (paperback) | ISBN 9781493067220 (epub)
Subjects: LCSH: Outdoor cooking. | Cast-iron cookware. | Camping—Equipment
  and supplies.
Classification: LCC TX823 .C68 2023 (print) | LCC TX823 (ebook) | DDC
  641.5/782—dc23/eng/20221202
LC record available at https://lccn.loc.gov/2022046976
LC ebook record available at https://lccn.loc.gov/2022046977

♾™ The paper used in this publication meets the minimum requirements of American
National Standard for Information Sciences—Permanence of Paper for Printed Library
Materials, ANSI/NISO Z39.48-1992.

To Max Phelps, our colleague in publishing from the draft of our first book nearly three decades ago. You have been a wise counselor, a staunch advocate, and, most importantly, a constant friend throughout this amazing life journey.

For we brought nothing into the world, and we cannot take anything out of the world. But if we have food and clothing, with these we will be content.

1 Timothy 6:7-8 (ESV)

CONTENTS

ACKNOWLEDGMENTS

We are in our third decade as authors for FalconGuides. There have been many changes in the industry from when we completed that first draft many years ago. But two individuals have been a part of the ride for a long time now: David Legere, Editorial Director, and Max Phelps, Director of Outdoor Sales. Dave, you have our ongoing gratitude for your relentlessly enthusiastic support of our work. And Max, we would have never even made it to that first edition of *Lipsmackin' Backpackin'* without you. Thank you.

We would also like to express our appreciation to the editing and production crew for *Lipsmackin' Cast Iron Cookin'*, in particular Felicity Tucker, Production Editor, and Elissa Curcio, our copyeditor. Thanks to you both for making our book shine. Finally, we extend our gratitude toward all of our contributors, but there are three in particular who were essential to making the book what it is: Robert Dowdy, Ken Spiegel, and Jim Rausch. Not only did you go above and beyond by providing many top-tier cast iron recipes, but you were also wonderful to work with during the testing and editing process. Thank you for your whole-hearted support and for the great attitude that went along with it.

INTRODUCTION

It wasn't long ago that cooking with cast iron was generally viewed as a quaint throwback to the pioneer days. If you did happen to own cast iron, it was likely some hand-me-down from antiquity and used only when all the "conventional" cookware was waiting in the sink or dishwasher to be cleaned. In fact, we had never even seen a Dutch oven in action until the mid-2000s after our sons became Scouts. We were surprised to find cast iron in widespread use on nearly every troop campout and amazed at the cooking magic being made. But what we were witnessing on Scout outings seemed to be the exception because the majority of people we knew outside of Scouting weren't regularly cooking with cast iron at home.

My, have times changed. The turn in cast iron popularity began about a decade ago and really accelerated during the pandemic years as people spent more time cooking at home, exploring new options and techniques. Now most everyone is familiar at some level with cast iron cooking, and cookware manufacturers have barely been able to keep up with demand.

But what would drive the resurgence in this form of cooking? We can provide an educated answer because we went through the awakening ourselves and, within a few years after, authored five books based in part on cast iron cooking. To cut to the essence: *cast iron cookware is incredibly versatile*. You will find no other form of cooking utensil that can compare. At home, cast iron can be used over any type of cook surface, in any form of oven, and on any grill. Outdoors, you can use *the same* cookware over a campfire, grill, or camp stove, or simply heaped with hot coals.

Let's talk a little more about cooking outside. Thinking about taking along that expensive conventional cook pot with the glass lid for some outdoor cooking? Probably not. How about putting your high-end non-stick fry pan over the unpredictable flames of a campfire? If that doesn't cause second thoughts, it should. When was the last time you piled red hot coals on the lid of your seasonal roasting pan? We would guess never. And would you feel comfortable leaving your conventional cooking gear outdoors . . . across a week of camping . . . sitting on the ground . . . in rain or snow? Right.

For cooking, it's their bulk that makes cast iron ovens and skillets such great devices. Thick walls evenly distribute heat for uniform cooking while reducing the chance of burning. Heavy lids on the ovens trap moisture, preventing food from drying out while cooking. And cast iron retains heat long after the skillet or oven is off the flame, keeping food warm throughout mealtime, even in cold weather.

To be fair, it isn't that functional substitutes can't be found that serve some of the various duties of cast iron when cooking outdoors. But no other cookware performs *as many functions* while being *as durable*. Consider the Dutch oven: it can easily serve as a browning pan, cook pot, fryer, slow cooker, roaster, bread maker, popcorn machine, or an oven for baking pies. You can even make ice cream in a Dutch oven! Cast iron skillets are a close second to Dutch ovens in camp cooking functionality. Like their cousin, cast iron skillets can also be used over, or in, any heat source, so no need to worry about warping or melting. They are not only great for all forms of frying but also excellent for preparing stews, pan pastas, desserts, and even breads. There are many interesting and useful variations to cast iron cooking in the outdoor setting.

Convinced that cast iron cooking is what you want and need on your next outdoor excursion? Awesome, because you should be. But now what? Well, that's where this book comes in. *Lipsmackin' Cast Iron Cookin'* is built on tried-and-true recipes from some of the most experienced and practical outdoor camp chefs in the business. Each recipe is clearly written and has been thoroughly tested and refined to ensure predictable and outstanding results, all while addressing the specific challenges associated with outdoor cooking.

And if you're new to camp cooking and are unfamiliar with using cast iron cookware, or if you simply need a refresher, you'll find all the information you'll need in the front matter of this book for guiding you safely, efficiently, and with confidence. Further help is in the appendices for finding, measuring, and converting ingredients, discovering new recipes, locating gear, and learning low-impact cooking techniques.

Whatever your experience level with cast iron cooking, this book is your gateway to producing culinary masterpieces with your cookware. May new and wonderfully enticing aromas be found drifting from your campsite, drawing in your fellow campers to the special camaraderie that can only be found outdoors!

Christine and Tim Conners
Tucson, Arizona

Planning and Preparing Your Meals

The foundation of the Lipsmackin' series of cookbooks has always been outstanding recipes created by some of the world's most skilled outdoor chefs. While the recipes take center stage, what may not be as obvious is that all of them made the cut only after careful screening and testing according to specific attributes essential to any great outdoor recipe: taste, variety, and simplicity. It is upon these three attributes that *Lipsmackin' Cast Iron Cookin'* is built as well.

To address simplicity, this book primarily uses recipes that are easily and predictably prepared in the campground setting. But for taste, variety, *and* simplicity—all three—planning is as important as preparation. This chapter discusses how to use this book most effectively for both planning and preparation while providing foundational knowledge essential to further developing skills in both.

The Camp Dutch Oven

A few words are warranted up front about the star of the show. Not that cast iron frying pans aren't stellar performers in their own right, but the Dutch oven is the glamour boy here, and you'll see why after a few recipes. When you're camping, however, you typically won't be using a standard Dutch oven of the style usually found in the home kitchen. Instead, you'll be doing most of your cooking with a *camp* Dutch oven. Compared to a standard Dutch oven, the camp version sports two essential design differences that vastly extend its versatility when cooking outdoors.

First, a camp Dutch oven typically stands on three squat legs instead of resting on a flat-bottom surface. The legs allow the oven to cook over a bed of coals without coming into contact with them. This provides more uniform heat distribution within the oven while preventing charring of the food that would otherwise occur due to direct contact of the oven with the coals. Second, the lid of a camp oven is flanged around its perimeter to allow coals to be placed across the top of the oven without sliding off. Coals on the lid are what allow a camp Dutch oven to truly function as an oven by creating a surrounding heat source, underneath and on top, for the food inside.

It should be noted that camp Dutch ovens can absolutely do double-duty by serving in the home kitchen, just as standard Dutch ovens work fine in camp. Just keep in mind that a camp Dutch oven generally needs to rest on a tray when used in a conventional kitchen oven to prevent its legs from sliding in between the rungs of the oven rack. And a standard

Dutch oven, because it lacks legs, must rest on a grate or other device to keep it elevated from the heat source. Also make note that a standard Dutch oven, with its domed cover, doesn't easily support coals on the lid. So the standard Dutch oven design generally best serves in a camp setting as a robust cooking pot as opposed to an actual oven.

Recipe Categories

There are as many ways to organize a cookbook as there are eating styles and preferences. The approach that appears to satisfy most people, and the one used in this book, is to begin by organizing entrees according to the meal category they best belong to: breakfast, lunch, or dinner. Those recipes that could not readily be tagged as "main dish" were grouped into three other primary categories: side dishes, breads, and snacks and desserts.

A special note is warranted regarding the lunch section, which has been constructed around the premise that campers are either on the move at midday or kicking back, siesta style—neither situation making a challenging menu attractive. And so noontime meals have been selected based on ease of preparation and cleanup. Only those recipes with an estimated total preparation time of an hour or less were included in the lunch category. Some of the lunch recipes also call for a campfire as the heat source, with the premise that the early campfire will have died down by late morning to produce a gentle bed of embers perfect for cooking. Of course, if you want to prepare a more involved meal at midday, consult the recipes in the dinner section, most of which perform equally well at the noon hour.

Category System

This book uses a category system that allows you to rapidly assess the most appropriate recipe options when planning a menu for the campground. Five key considerations are typically used when developing a list of candidate recipes: (1) the equipment available, (2) the number of people to prepare for, (3) the time available to prepare the meal, (4) the level of skill required to achieve good results, and (5) any special nutrition requirements.

To help ensure you pack the proper gear along with the food, the required cooking method necessary *in camp*—camp Dutch oven, standard Dutch oven, skillet, or pie iron—is indicated by corresponding icons. The icon system that identifies the required cooking method, located at the top of each recipe, is defined in the following table. With one glance, the icon system provides a rapid introduction to the primary tools and heat sources required for each recipe. Using the icon system, you can move quickly past the recipes that aren't an option.

Cooking Method Icons

	Camp Dutch oven with coals or other heat source
	Standard Dutch oven on camp stove or other heat source
	Skillet on camp stove or other heat source
	Pie iron over campfire or other heat source

As discussed in the preceding section, recipes are first grouped at the top level by meal category, forming the core chapters of the book. But from there, the recipes have been subgrouped by the required cooking method, then by the number of servings, followed by the preparation time, and, finally, by the challenge level. Number of servings, preparation time, and challenge level are listed prominently at the head of each recipe.

For campers looking specifically for meatless options, a **V-LO** icon is used to identify the recipe as lacto-ovo vegetarian, free of meat but containing dairy and/or egg products. For recipes free of not only meat but also dairy and egg, an icon simply indicating **V** marks the selection as vegan.

Servings

For consistency, serving estimates assume the target audience to be active adults on a moderate caloric intake. Serving sizes were adjusted upward as credit for healthier recipes and downward for those with less desirable nutrition characteristics. Adjust your estimates according to your specific situation, keeping in mind that activity level, richness of the meal, food preferences, snacking, and weather will all influence the actual number of servings you'll obtain from each recipe.

Many established campgrounds impose a limit to the number of campers at each site, and the recipes take this into consideration: The maximum number of servings found in this book rarely exceeds eight to ten. However, it's a straightforward task to multiply recipes to meet the needs of larger groups. Some recipes permit a significant increase (or decrease) in the number of servings using the original equipment specified in the recipe. For instance, a recipe that calls for a Dutch oven that produces half a dozen servings might be able to squeeze in several more just by adding more ingredients.

Preparation Time

Total preparation time under pleasant weather conditions has been estimated for each recipe. Usually rounded to the nearest quarter hour, this value includes the time required to prepare the heat source (if required) through to serving the dish. It is assumed that the chef will follow the preparation steps in parallel and use assistance whenever possible. For instance, while the coals are starting or meat is browning, other preparation steps can often be accomplished simultaneously. The recipes are written to best take advantage of this.

Challenge Level

A three-tier system has been used to assign a challenge level to each recipe: "easy," "moderate," or "difficult." The decision was based on the preparation and cleanup effort required in camp, the sensitivity of the cooking technique to variation, and the attention to care necessary to avoid injury. Most of the recipes in this book have been tagged as "easy," an important quality especially for the camp setting, where simplicity is definitely welcome.

Preparation Instructions

Instructions for each recipe include a list of ingredients, carefully selected to create less waste or leftovers of key items. Also included are step-by-step directions, each logically grouped and presented in numerical sequence. The use of numerical sequencing in the preparation steps is intended to help the chef stay focused and to assist in the assignment of specific tasks to other campers able to lend a hand. This is especially important for larger groups, where the delegation of tasks is an important component of smooth and successful meal preparation. Nearly all recipes in this book are prepared completely in camp, requiring no at-home preparation steps in advance.

Heating instructions are clear and consistent and provide high probability of success under a wide range of cooking conditions. For extra precision with camp Dutch oven recipes, an exact number of standard-size briquettes (coals) is specified for use on the lid and under the oven.

If an actual baking temperature is required, say, to modify a Dutch oven recipe or to adapt it to a larger or smaller oven, use the conversion chart below to make the transformation by converting the specified coal

Coal-Temperature Conversion Chart

		Oven Temperature					
		325°F	350°F	375°F	400°F	425°F	450°F
8"	Total Briquettes	15	16	17	18	19	20
	On Lid	10	11	11	12	13	14
	Underneath Oven	5	5	6	6	6	6
10"	Total Briquettes	19	21	23	25	27	29
	On Lid	13	14	16	17	18	19
	Underneath Oven	6	7	7	8	9	10
12"	Total Briquettes	23	25	27	29	31	33
	On Lid	16	17	18	19	21	22
	Underneath Oven	7	8	9	10	10	11
14"	Total Briquettes	30	32	34	36	38	40
	On Lid	20	21	22	24	25	26
	Underneath Oven	10	11	12	12	13	14
16"	Total Briquettes	37	39	41	43	45	47
	On Lid	25	26	27	28	29	30
	Underneath Oven	12	13	14	15	16	17

Dutch Oven Diameter

count and Dutch oven size back into a temperature value. This conversion chart, based on data from Lodge Manufacturing, is very reliable when cooking with cast iron stoves under pleasant weather conditions and using standard-size, high-quality briquettes, fresh from the charcoal starter. The chart is also useful for selecting the appropriate kitchen oven temperature when preparing your favorite camp recipes at home.

Required Equipment

A list of cooking equipment required at camp follows the ingredients. For reasons of practicality, not every item necessary to prepare a recipe is listed. For example, a cooler or refrigeration device is obviously essential for keeping perishable foods safe. It is assumed that one is always available for use. Other gear assumed to be basic equipment residing in any camp kitchen includes the following:

- Cook pot
- Food thermometer
- Measuring cups and spoons
- Can opener
- Cutting and paring knives
- Cutting boards
- Long-handled wooden spoons
- Long-handled ladle
- Food-grade greasing agent, such as vegetable oil
- Serving plates, utensils, cups, napkins, and paper towels
- Washbasins, scrub pads, dish detergent, and towels
- Hand sanitizer
- Work and serving tables
- Heavy barbecue gloves

It is also assumed that all necessary tools and equipment are available for preparing and managing the heat source required for each selected recipe, such as briquettes, coal starter, coal tray, tongs, and lid lifter when using a Dutch oven. When a recipe's equipment necessities go beyond the list of these basics, those requirements are listed with each recipe to head off any surprises in camp.

When bowls and skillets are specified for some recipes, "small," "medium-size," and "large" are used to approximate the capacity to do the job. By having a range of sizes of utensils available at camp, you'll never find yourself in a pickle during food preparation. If ever in doubt on utensil size requirements, err on the side of larger capacity.

Regarding camp Dutch ovens, a 10-inch/4-quart size is specified for most of the Dutch oven recipes in the book. This size is perfect for producing six to eight servings and is perhaps the most versatile oven to purchase for camping if you currently don't own one. Less frequently, a 12-inch/6-quart or, rarely, a deep 14-inch/10-quart is called for because the larger internal volume is necessary for some roasting and baking jobs. And a lone recipe calls for a smaller 8-inch/2-quart oven, a good size for rich desserts or fewer number of servings. Camp Dutch ovens of sizes other than these are also available; while these can be handy when adapting a dish for a different number of servings, they are not required to use this book.

For standard Dutch ovens—that is, the oven style without legs—sizes are generally referred to in the industry by volume only, not diameter. Sizes from 1 to 7 quarts are typical. A medium-size standard Dutch oven of about 5 to 6 quarts is perhaps the most flexible in the camp setting. In fact, the medium size is appropriate for all recipes in this book calling for a standard Dutch oven.

Owning a range of oven sizes is useful for convenience, but you could get by with only a couple of sizes to prepare all the Dutch oven recipes in this book, keeping in mind that larger ovens can almost always be used for smaller recipes provided that the coal count or heat source is adjusted accordingly. And a camp Dutch oven can usually improvise for a standard Dutch oven design by being flexible with the heat source, for example, by using coals under the oven as opposed to using a camp stove.

Some recipes call for the use of a gadget known as a pie iron, the camp version of the kitchen panini press. Made from cast iron and situated on the end of a long handle, pie irons are simple devices designed to toast stuffed sandwiches and shell-based filled desserts directly in or over the campfire. They can be found in a variety of shapes and sizes, but the recipes in this book use what is arguably the most common: a rectangular design about 4 inches on a side.

Options and Tips

Interesting cooking options are provided for many of the recipes. Options differ from the main instructions and produce alternate endings to the recipe. Options included with a recipe are shown separately from the main preparation steps.

Likewise, contributors occasionally offer helpful tips that can assist the camp chef with purchasing ingredients or preparing the recipe in some way. As with options, tips are listed separately from the main body of the recipe.

Contributor Information

Rounding out each recipe is information about the contributors. These are the field experts who made the book possible. You'll learn their names and the places of residence they call home. Many of our contributors included anecdotes and stories as well. Useful and often humorous, you'll find these before each recipe.

Supplemental Information for the Camp Chef

Additional information is included in the front and back sections of the book to assist with the challenge of outdoor cooking. An important section on safety (later in this chapter) highlights the most common risks found in the camp kitchen and what can be done to help reduce the probability of an accident. Be safe. Review this material, especially if you are new to camp cooking.

Hand in hand with safety comes skill. An expert camp cook is far less likely to inflict injury or illness to themselves or their fellow campers. A section on basic skills (also later in this chapter) reviews the competencies that outdoor cooks should seek to understand and master.

The appendices cover a wide variety of helpful reference information: kitchen measurement conversions, sources of camp cooking gear and ingredients, a bibliography of additional books and information on outdoor cooking, and techniques for reducing the environmental impact of camp cooking.

Healthy Pairings

Wise choices and moderation are the keys to maintaining a healthy diet in camp, and these begin with the planning process. When choosing recipes that lean toward higher fats and sugars, balance your meals with light salads or fresh vegetables. Instead of pairing a heavy entree with a rich dessert, select a lighter after-dinner option, such as fresh fruit. If everyone's favorite decadent dessert is on the menu, choose a less rich dinner to go with it. Avoid serving multiple courses at a meal, which not only complicates meal planning and cleanup but also contributes to overeating.

Between meals, have plenty of healthy snacks available instead of fatty and sugary cookies and candy. Bananas, oranges, clementines, peaches, nectarines, plums, apples, and carrots are all easy to store and serve while in camp. Nuts and tortilla chips and salsa make for favorite between-meal snacks.

Camp Cooking Safety

The outdoor kitchen presents some of the more significant hazards that a camper will face, and yet the risks are often taken for granted. Most people have learned to successfully manage dangers in the home kitchen through caution and experience. But *camp* cooking presents many new and unique hazards that, if not appreciated and controlled, can cause severe injury or illness. The following information on cooking safety highlights the most common risks found in the camp kitchen and what can be done to help reduce the probability of an accident.

While the goal should always be zero accidents, minor injuries, including cuts and burns, are not uncommon. Keep the first-aid kit handy for these. Never acceptable, however, are more serious injuries or food-borne illness. Extreme care and caution should always be used to prevent accidents that could otherwise send you or your diners to the doctor or hospital.

Be careful! Searing hot metal can char skin instantly. Sharp knifes can go deep into a finger before the brain has time to register what is happening. Heavy cast iron dropped on a foot can smash unprotected bones. Harmful bacteria left alive due to improper cooking can leave one so ill that the body barely clings to life.

Learn to respect *every* step of the cooking process. Always think about what you are preparing to do and ask yourself, "Is this safe?" If you don't believe it is, or even if you are uncomfortable for reasons you don't understand, trust your instinct. Stop and determine how to do the job better, either by using more appropriate techniques and equipment or by asking others for assistance or advice.

And don't try to mimic the chefs you see on video. That fancy speed chopping might look impressive, but it's dangerous if you don't know what you're doing. Move slowly and methodically. No matter how hungry your crew may be, no meal is worth compromising health and well-being.

With care and attention, any cooking risk can be managed to an acceptable level. The following list of guidelines for safety will help you do just that.

Supervision and Assistance

- First and foremost, a responsible adult must always carefully supervise the cooking activities of inexperienced adults or children, even more so when heat, sharp utensils, or raw meat is involved.

- The picnic table, ubiquitous in most campground settings, often serves as a useful surface for many functions: cooking, serving, dining, and cleaning being the most obvious. But because the picnic table is already the center of such a busy area, it's best to move the cooking to a less chaotic part of camp to avoid unnecessary distraction or interference.

- When setting up your camp kitchen, structure the preparation area according to work flow to minimize the chances of your assistants running into either you or each other, especially when carrying sharp knives, hot food, or heavy equipment. Give everyone plenty of room to work.

- When cooking for larger groups, the workload will increase, as will the probability of falling behind schedule. If you find yourself trailing, don't rush to catch up. The chances of accident and injury will only increase. And don't be a martyr, suffering silently under the burden. You'll only fatigue yourself all the more quickly. Instead, immediately enlist help from other skilled members of your group to help get the meal preparation back on track.

Food Poisoning

- Ensure that recipes containing raw meat or eggs are thoroughly cooked. Use a food thermometer to take several readings at various locations throughout the food being prepared. Minimum safe cooking temperatures vary by food type, but 165°F is high enough to kill all common food-borne pathogens. Use this value when in doubt.

- Cold and wet weather can significantly lower the temperature of the heat source and cookware. To compensate, prepare to increase the length of cooking time or, if using a Dutch oven, the number of coals. Windy weather can have an unpredictable effect on a Dutch oven, the temperature within the oven sometimes becoming uneven. The use of a food thermometer is especially recommended in all cases of adverse weather when cooking raw meat or eggs.

- Care should be taken when handling raw meat or eggs to prevent cross-contamination of other foods such as raw vegetables. When preparing raw meats, cutting surfaces and utensils should be dedicated *only* to this task or thoroughly washed with detergent prior to use for other purposes. Avoid the mistake of placing just-cooked food into an unwashed bowl or tray used earlier to mix or hold raw meat or eggs.

- In the potential confusion of a larger group setting, with several assistants working together in the camp kitchen, it is important to clearly communicate to the others if work surfaces or utensils are being used to prepare raw meat or eggs. Otherwise, the equipment may be used improperly, leading to cross-contamination of the food.

- Raw meat and eggs should be tightly sealed in a container or ziplock bag and placed in a cooler until ready to use. To avoid cross-contamination, keep these items in their own cooler, separate from raw fruits and vegetables, cheese, beverages, or any other items that will not eventually be cooked at high temperature.

- Drinking ice must be stored in its own clean and dedicated cooler. *Ice from a cooler used for storing raw meats and eggs should never be used in beverages.*

- Sanitize your hands and work area with antibacterial cleaners appropriate for the kitchen both before and after the meal.

- Using soap and water or hand sanitizer, thoroughly clean your hands *immediately* after you've handled raw meat or eggs and *before* touching any other cooking instruments or ingredients. If you must repeatedly touch raw meat or eggs during preparation, then repeatedly sanitize your hands before handling anything else. Be sure that you and the rest of the kitchen crew are compulsive about this. It's that important.

- All food that could potentially spoil, including leftovers, should be kept on ice. To prolong the life of your ice, store coolers in a shady, cool, secure location, with lids tightly sealed. Covering the coolers with sleeping bags or blankets on a warm day will further insulate them.

- Be sure that water used for cooking has been properly treated or purified before using. Do not simply assume that any water from a camp spigot is safe to drink. Ask camp officials if you are unsure.

Cuts, Burns, and Broken Bones

- Cutting utensils are inherently dangerous, and it goes without saying that they should be handled with care. Dull blades can be more dangerous than sharper instruments. Dull knife blades unintentionally slip much more easily when slicing or chopping and can quickly end up in the side of your finger instead of the food you're cutting. Maintaining the sharpness of knife blades will help ensure they do what you expect. When slicing and chopping, always keep hands and fingers away from the underside of the cutting edge or from in front of the blade tip.

- Do not share a cutting board concurrently with one of your kitchen colleagues. You could end up injuring each other. Instead, take turns using the board or employ a second one for use.

- Extreme care should be taken when cleaning and storing sharp kitchen instruments. A knife at the bottom of a washbasin filled with cloudy water is a potential booby trap for the unlucky dishwasher who doesn't know it's there. Don't leave knives hidden in soapy water. The same holds true when storing sharp utensils after cleaning. Knives, in particular, should be sheathed in a holder when placed back in storage.

- When using a cookstove to prepare food in a pot or frying pan, be sure that long handles are turned away from the edge of the stove or table to prevent inadvertently knocking over the hot cookware and spilling the contents.

- Do not use a frying pan or cook pot that is too large for the cookstove. If a pot or pan significantly overhangs the burner grill, it could topple. If your setup is unstable, switch to a smaller pot or pan or find a larger stove.

- Never use a flimsy table for cooking. It could buckle under the weight and send the hot stove and food flying. Any table used for cooking must be sturdy.

- Use protective gear, such as heavy leather barbecue gloves, on both hands when handling hot coals or tending a cooking fire. Ensure that the gloves are long enough to protect your forearms. If you fail to regularly use heavy protective gloves in these situations, the probability is high that you will eventually suffer a nasty burn. Closed-top shoes are also required. The top of your bare foot won't quickly forget a red-hot briquette landing snugly between your sandal straps.

- Cast iron cookware can be heavy. But a large Dutch oven or frying pan filled to the brim with hot food can be *very* heavy . . . and dangerous. Wear heatproof gloves and closed-top footwear when handling hot and loaded cast iron. And if the cookware is too heavy for you to safely manage alone, swallow your pride and ask for help.

- Cast iron retains heat for a long time after it is removed from the coals. This is a great quality for keeping food warm during mealtime, but it also sets the stage for burn injuries to the unsuspecting. Before moving any cast iron with unprotected hands after the meal, carefully check to be sure the metal has cooled sufficiently. If it hasn't, or if you're unsure, use heatproof gloves.

Fire Safety

- All cooking must be performed in a fire-safe area of camp, clear of natural combustibles like dry leaves, grass, and trees, and away from wooden structures. When cooking directly on the ground using coals, select a durable area covered in fireproof material such as rock, gravel, or bare earth. Be sure to follow any special open-fire restrictions established for your region. If unsure, ask camp officials about this when checking in. Always have a large container of water handy to douse any flames that may escape your fire-safe perimeter.

- When using a cookstove, keep loose and combustible items such as dish towels, plastic bags, aprons, long sleeves, baggy clothing, and hair away from the flame.

- Cooking fires require special attention to avoid injury. Keep the fire just large enough to do the job. Use long-handled tongs when managing foods in the fire. If cooking above a fire using a grill grate, ensure that the grate is strong and sturdy enough to handle the weight of the cookware and food that you're placing on it. Be sure the fire is cold out before leaving camp.

- Hot coals on the ground present a potential hazard during cooking, but especially afterward. With a Dutch oven off the heat, and with the coals ashed over, the threat lurking in your cooking area might go unnoticed. Notify your fellow campers of the danger of hot coals on the ground. Keep the area off-limits to all but essential personnel until the coals expire. Once the coals have fully cooled, discard the ash in a fire-safe manner appropriate for your camp.

- Unless they are vented, noxious fumes from a camp stove or burning coals will rise and concentrate within the apex of any roof under which cooking is performed. So when a kitchen tent or tarp structure is used for cooking in camp, the apex must be substantially higher than a tall person's head, and with walls open and well ventilated on all sides. When cooking in a kitchen tent, be especially diligent to maintain a large fire-safe perimeter around the cooking area. Never attempt to cook in a *sleeping* tent. The fully enclosed walls will concentrate deadly gases and cause asphyxiation, or the tent floor or walls could rapidly catch fire and trap the occupants. A standard picnic canopy with a low ceiling or partially enclosed side walls is also unsafe for cooking because the apex is at head height and the walls are often too low or poorly ventilated.

- Do not use a barbecue grill in a kitchen tent. A flare-up could create a fire hazard, and any concentration of smoke could be dangerous.

Allergies and Special Diets

When planning a menu for a group outing, be sure to consider food allergies or health issues that might require special dietary restrictions. Selecting recipes that meet everyone's tastes and requirements may seem impossible in these circumstances, but many recipes can be modified to meet dietary requirements while satisfying everyone else in the group. This approach can be far easier than attempting to adhere to a parallel special-requirements menu.

Wild Animals

Animals searching for food scraps and garbage can pose a danger to the camp environment, through either aggression or disease. Unattended dirty dishes, unsecured garbage, food items and coolers left in the open— all of these will eventually attract unwanted animal attention and can create a major problem, especially in bear country. Wildlife that gains access to such goodies will surely come back for more, placing these animals at risk of harm along with the people who must then interact with them or remove them. A camp kept neat and clean, with food and garbage properly stored and secured, is far less attractive to the local fauna. Practice low-impact camping principles and adhere to any food storage regulations unique to your area or camp.

No list can cover every potential danger, and this is surely no exception. But by learning to cook with a mind fixated on safety, few circumstances will catch you ill prepared or by surprise.

Basic Skills for the Camp Chef

Great camp cooking might seem magical, but it does not come by accident. A strong foundation in the fundamentals of outdoor cookery will make it all the more likely you'll be successful. With this in mind, the following sections cover the essential skills.

Planning for the Obvious . . . and the Unexpected

- If you are a camp-cooking neophyte, keep your menu simple, especially when preparing food for larger crowds. Raise the challenge level only after becoming more skilled and confident in your abilities. Taking on more work than one can manage is a common camp-kitchen mistake, and the botched meal that results is sure to disappoint not only the one doing the work but any hungry stomachs depending on the chef.

- Many recipes serve admirably as "one-pot" meals. These are perfect for newer chefs, where simplicity is welcome. Unless you are looking for a real challenge, avoid complex, multi-pot meals and rely instead on a one-pot entree and a simple side or two, such as fresh salad and sliced bread. Aluminum "steam table pans" make excellent and inexpensive containers for serving large quantities of salads and breads to larger groups.

- After the gear is purchased, groceries account for the majority of cost on many outings. However, now is not the time to be overly frugal. Cost cutting can be taken to an extreme, with ingredients of such low quality that it's painfully obvious, meal after meal. Consider spending the additional money on quality ingredients. You'll appreciate the difference once at camp.

- The ability to multitask is a hallmark of great chefs, and it becomes even more important when dealing with large quantities of ingredients or when replicating recipes. But don't act as the Lone Ranger when cooking for large groups. Enlist help and divide kitchen duties to lighten the load while cooking and cleaning. Discuss roles and responsibilities in advance so there is no confusion when it comes time to engage. The recipes in this book use numerical sequencing for the instructions. Use these to best assign tasks to the helpers.

- They are often enthusiastic to assist, but inexperienced adults and younger children require more supervision. Make sure you can manage the additional workload when assigning tasks to the tenderfoots. Some don't know a can opener from a pizza cutter or won't have a clue as to how to crack an egg. When cooking under trying circumstances, it may be better to leave the inexperienced chefs out of the kitchen altogether.

- The younger the children, the more they tend to openly grumble about their food, even when it is obviously awesome to everyone else. And after a long evening of cooking in camp, complaining is the last thing you want to hear. A powerful way to avoid this is to include all of your fellow campers, especially the younger ones, in the meal-planning process. By giving them a voice, they become stakeholders in the meal's success and are more likely to enjoy the results.

- Read through and understand the *entire* recipe before commencing preparation. You are far less likely to make a critical mistake by doing so. And be sure to have everything you need before starting a recipe by first gathering all ingredients and cooking utensils to your work area.

- When planning your menu, don't ignore the flexibility of the camp Dutch oven, which can be used in place of a frying pan, grill grate, or cook pot for many recipes that otherwise require one. If a camp stove, barbecue grill, or wood fire will be unavailable for your favorite recipes at your next outing, consider adapting these dishes to the circumstances. A camp Dutch oven and a bag of briquettes can probably do the job easily and admirably.

- Foul weather adds a powerful variable to the camp cooking equation. And bugs and wild animals further distract by keeping the cook on the defensive. Prior to any outing, weather and critters should be considered and planned for appropriately. Be realistic about what you can handle under the circumstances likely to be encountered. The more trying the conditions, the simpler the menu should be.

- Even the most foolproof dish sometimes ends its short life tragically dumped in the dirt by fate or accident. Whatever the cause may be, always have a Plan B at the ready, whether boxed macaroni or a map to the nearest grocery store. At some point you are likely to need it.

Tailoring Your Camp Kitchen

- Once arriving at camp, give careful thought to your kitchen area. Set up the work tables in a quiet, level location. Choose an area with a durable surface. Otherwise, all the foot traffic will wear down grasses and sensitive plant growth. Avoid muddy or low-lying areas, especially if rain is in the forecast. If using a campfire or camp Dutch oven, the cooking area should be adjacent to the camp kitchen so that a close eye can be kept on the situation. When using coals or a campfire, a fire-safe perimeter must be established around the cooking area, free of all combustibles.

- Consider your work flow and logically position the cooking area, work tables, serving tables, storage bins, coolers, and trash containers to minimize cross traffic (and collisions) within the kitchen area. If possible, position the main kitchen away from the serving area so that hungry diners don't get in the way of the chefs as they go about finishing their tasks. In fact, a good option is to use the campground's picnic table for serving, while keeping the kitchen area itself well clear of that busy hot spot.

- Many, but certainly not all, campgrounds provide a barbecue grill in each individual campsite. Before structuring your menu around the presumed presence of a camp grill, confirm with the campground office that one will indeed be available if you are unsure. Bring along a wire brush to clean and scrape the grill's grate before using, and pack your own portable campfire grate as backup in the event that the actual camp grill turns out to be in disrepair. Portable grates are inexpensive and easy to find in the camping section at larger retailers.

- When cooking for large groups, bring along extra mixing bowls and other less expensive utensils, such as knives, measuring cups, and long-handled mixing spoons. That way any assistants will never be without the tools needed to do their job. And always have several cutting boards available. Lack of adequate cutting equipment is a common bottleneck in the camp kitchen.

- Have plenty of sturdy folding tables when cooking for large groups. Otherwise, if table space is very limited, and some of the food preparation is relegated out of necessity to the serving area or to the ground, the process can quickly become unhygienic, inefficient, and frustrating. Keep in mind that extra table space will also be required for serving the food.

Reduce, Reuse, Recycle

- Avoid waste by setting out only the number of serving plates, bowls, and utensils required for the meal. Consider asking your campmates to reuse their serving ware for other courses, such as salad or dessert. Have a permanent marker available for writing names on disposable plastic cups so that these can be reused. Better yet, maintain and use personal mess kits when camping, or, at the least, bring along durable drinking cups from home with names marked on them.

- Some serving ware, though disposable, is robust enough to pass through the dishwasher. If this is the case for your situation, consider using a bin, box, aluminum steam table pan, or bag to collect used utensils once they've been rinsed. Then clean them in bulk later, in the dishwasher at home, for future reuse.

Managing the Heat

- When using a skillet or Dutch oven on a grate over a campfire, the cooking temperature is much easier to control if the flames are low and the fire has a solid, level bed of embers. If you plan to use open fire as your heat source, start the campfire long before mealtime to give it time to die down and stabilize.

- Select a high-quality briquette of standard size when using charcoal with a Dutch oven. Extra-large or small briquettes, or even embers from the campfire, can also work, but their nonstandard size will make it more challenging to achieve proper results when following a cookbook, such as this one, that specifies exact coal counts based on a standard briquette size.

- Many Dutch oven recipes with a high liquid content, such as stews, can easily tolerate inexact briquette counts. Because of this, irregular-size coals from the campfire can be readily used as the fuel source instead. By using embers from the campfire, the additional twenty minutes or so otherwise required to start briquettes from scratch is eliminated. Reducing the preparation time in this manner also makes many Dutch oven dinner recipes a viable option at lunchtime, even when the schedule is tight.

- Intense heat is transferred through the walls of a Dutch oven in those areas where coals come into *direct contact* with the metal. Food touching the walls on the inside surface of these hot spots will likely char. With coals usually on the lid by default, it is imperative that tall foods, such as rising breads or roasts, are cooked in a Dutch oven deep enough to keep the food from contacting the lid's inside surface. Below the oven, the briquettes must be positioned to not directly touch the metal's underside, or the food on the floor of the oven will probably burn. If these simple rules are followed, you should never find it necessary to scrape carbon from your breads or expensive cuts of meat.

- Briquettes often clump together when placing or moving the oven during cooking. They sometimes congregate on the lid, but their sly gatherings usually occur under the oven, where their unruly behavior is more difficult to observe. The problem is that the clumping can create hot spots that produce uneven cooking, especially while baking. To prevent this, redistribute the wayward coals as necessary, especially under the oven, and rotate the oven one-quarter turn over the briquettes every fifteen minutes or so. At the same time, use a lid lifter to carefully rotate the lid one-quarter turn relative to the base.

- Heat escapes quickly when the lid is raised from a Dutch oven. Tempting as it may be to continually peek at that cheesecake, don't do so unless necessary. You'll only lengthen the cooking time.

- Hot briquettes quickly fail when used directly on moist surfaces. Avoid this common mistake by placing your coals and oven on a metal tray or other durable, dry, fireproof surface, such as the flat side of a row of cinder blocks. A tray or hard surface prevents the oven from settling down into the soil and into direct contact with the coals under the oven, which could otherwise cause the food to char. Cooking on a tray or raised surface also protects the ground from scarring and makes ash cleanup and disposal easier once the coals expire.

- Always bring plenty of extra charcoal briquettes to cover contingencies. Food preparation may take longer than expected, requiring additional coals to complete the meal. Windy, cold, or wet weather can also greatly increase the number of coals required. Don't get caught with an empty bag of briquettes and half-baked food.

- Preheat the Dutch oven in recipes that require hot metal to properly kick-start the cooking process, such as when sautéing vegetables or browning meats. An exact coal count isn't essential for preheating the oven, with about two dozen briquettes generally adequate for the job. When browning or sautéing, all the coals go under the oven because the lid is unused. When preheating the oven for recipes requiring the lid, the coals should be distributed between the lid and under the oven. Use any unspent hot coals for subsequent cooking steps.

- Most recipes for the Dutch oven are remarkably resilient against overcooking. The heavy, tight-fitting lid helps trap moisture, which prevents food from drying out when left on the coals longer than it needs to be. However, as is true in the home kitchen, *baked* items require more precision for great results. So pay closer attention to temperature and timing when baking.

- When cooking with more than one Dutch oven at mealtime, stacking the ovens, one on top of the other, can be a useful technique if the cooking area is limited. This method also saves on briquettes, as the coals on the lid of the bottom oven also heat the bottom of the oven on top. But be aware that stacking complicates the preparation, requiring careful placement of the ovens and more attention to coal distribution and cooking times. For instance, you wouldn't want to place a dish that requires frequent stirring at the bottom of the stack. Nor would you stack a Dutch oven that uses a low coal count on top of one requiring a lot of briquettes. Stacking several ovens can also be more hazardous, as a taller tower becomes more prone to toppling. Plan carefully and be extra cautious when using stacks.

Dealing with the Weather

- When a coal-covered Dutch oven lid is lifted while the wind is stirring, or if the lid is bumped while lifting, you'll watch in helpless wonder as ash majestically floats down onto your food. It's a beautiful sight, like powdered sugar on a chocolate cake. Unfortunately, ash doesn't taste like powdered sugar. So avoid jarring the lid when lifting, and remove it immediately toward the downwind side. This will minimize your ash-to-food ratio.

- In very windy conditions, place your stove or Dutch oven behind a windscreen of some sort while cooking; otherwise, the food will be subjected to uneven heating, potentially burned in some areas and undercooked in others. A row of coolers or storage bins can serve handily as a windbreak. Dutch oven stands, purpose-built for cooking off the ground, often come with built-in windscreens.

- Very chilly or windy weather can present a real challenge to keeping food warm prior to serving. Foods cooked in the Dutch oven can be left inside the oven until served, as the heft of the oven itself is very effective at trapping and holding heat. Cooked foods can also be placed in aluminum steam table trays, covered with foil, then layered in dry dish towels for insulation. A gas grill with a cover is also effective. Even coolers holding a few hot rocks from around the perimeter of the fire can serve as warming ovens, provided the rocks aren't so hot as to melt the plastic.

- Perhaps the most challenging of all outdoor cooking situations in an open kitchen involves rain. In a heavy downpour, the only options may be to cease and desist to wait it out, serve no-cook foods instead, or move the camp kitchen to a fire-safe covered area. Never cook in a sleeping tent.

- When using Dutch ovens in the rain, large sheets of heavy-duty aluminum foil, tented loosely over the top of the oven and tray, can offer some protection in a pinch but are unlikely to shield completely during a cloudburst. A large barbecue grill with a lid can protect your oven from the rain, with a metal tray placed on the grill grate serving as the cook surface. And, once again, a Dutch oven stand with a windscreen could serve nicely, with the screen supporting sheets of heavy foil or a tray for keeping the rain off the coals.

- A camp kitchen tent is arguably the most comfortable option for cooking in wet weather, but good judgment is a must when choosing and using a kitchen tent because of the very real risk of asphyxiation and fire. See the section earlier in this chapter for important information on kitchen tent safety.

- Cooking with a Dutch oven in snow presents its own unique difficulties, but these are easily managed if planned for in advance. If the snow is deep and cannot be easily cleared, cook off the ground on a durable surface. For example, a metal tray on a concrete picnic table works well in this instance. A Dutch oven stand can also be very useful in the snow. If your camping area has a sturdy grill, you can use a tray placed on the grate. You can also arrange wood logs in the snow to securely support a metal tray for placing the Dutch oven. The flat surface of several cinder blocks also works well in this situation.

Cleaning Up

- Maintain a close eye on your food while cooking so that it doesn't burn. Charred grub is difficult to remove from cookware and requires more time, water, and detergent during cleanup. Preventing food from burning is perhaps the single most important step for making cleanup easier.

- A pair of large butler basins or storage containers, one filled with sudsy water, the other with rinse water, makes cleanup more efficient.

- A lining of heavy-duty foil or parchment paper in the Dutch oven is excellent for containing messes from gooey recipes. Once the foil or paper is removed following the meal, most of the glop goes with it, making cleanup much easier. Note that a liner is usually not suitable for recipes that require a lot of stirring, because the foil or paper can snag and tear.

- Cleaning greasy cookware and dishes with cold water can be a real challenge to one's patience. Use warm water to cut grease and make cleanup more rapid and hygienic. Place a pot of water over low heat on the stove or campfire to warm for this purpose while the meal is being served. The water will be hot once it's time for cleanup. Carefully pour the hot water into the wash bin, bringing it to a safe temperature with cold water as required.

- Use dishwashing liquid sparingly during cleanup, just enough to do the job. Use only detergents that are biodegradable. (Information specific to cleaning and storing cast iron can be found in the following section.)

- Dirty dishes left to lie will eventually attract bugs and wild animals. To avoid such interest, ensure that all cookware and utensils have been washed and rinsed before leaving camp during the day or when retiring for the evening.

- Dispose of wash and rinse water, also called "gray water," in a manner acceptable for your particular camp. Some camping areas have dedicated gray water disposal stations. Never dump gray water directly into a stream or lake.

Caring for Cast Iron

- For cleanup, cast iron cookware requires no more than a sponge or dish rag for wiping, a gentle nonmetallic scrub pad or spatula for scraping, warm water for washing, plenty of clean water for rinsing, and a towel for drying. *Metal* scouring pads can wear or remove your cookware's protective coating (also called its patina or seasoning) and should be avoided unless they have been purposely designed for cast iron. Only small amounts of detergent should be used, and then only when necessary, because excessive soap can degrade the cast iron's patina.

- The warmer the wash water, the more effectively grease can be cut by water alone. When grease is heavy or solidified, and the wash water cold, use a small amount of dish soap.

- Never use a dishwasher to clean your cast iron. The strong detergents in a dishwasher can remove so much coating that re-seasoning would be required.

- Some recipes challenge even the best nonstick coating, especially if the food is frozen when first placed in the cookware or accidentally charred while cooking. Soaking cookware in water is the usual remedy for tough stuck-on foods, but cast iron should not be left for long periods in plain water. Otherwise, the patina may weaken and rust could form. Instead, pour an inch or two of very hot water into the soiled cookware before the residue has a chance to harden. This is a very effective and nondamaging cleaning method. The stubborn food will begin to loosen after just a few minutes. Once the soak water cools to a safe temperature, the residue can be removed with a nonmetallic spatula or scrub pad and the cookware then cleaned and rinsed as usual.

- If a separate cook pot is unavailable to heat wash water, add a shallow pool of clean water to the soiled Dutch oven or skillet and then place it over the campfire, camp stove, or any remaining hot coals. Once the water is hot, *very carefully* move the cast iron to a safe location. As the metal cools to a temperature safe for cleaning, the food residue will have loosened and subsequent cleanup will be much easier.

- When cleaning or drying, *never* allow cast iron cookware to go completely dry over a fire. The cast iron won't melt or warp, but the patina can quickly turn to ash without the protective influence of the moisture.

- Avoid placing hot cast iron in cool water. The resulting thermal shock can warp or crack the metal. Wait for your cookware to cool to the touch before immersing it in wash water or pouring water into it.

- Use a long-handled wooden or silicone spoon for mixing and stirring in your Dutch oven. Occasional use of metal spoons is acceptable, but avoid sustained use of metal utensils, which can wear the patina over time.

- Rub or spray a thin layer of food-grade oil over the entire surface of your cookware, including the legs and handles, both before using and after each cleaning. Doing so *before* cooking will further build the durability and effectiveness of the nonstick coating. And doing so *after* cleaning will protect the patina and prevent rust during storage. Using paper towels to spread the oil makes the job easier and less messy. *If this important maintenance step is regularly neglected prior to cooking or long-term storage, the protective patina is likely to be damaged and rust can form.*

- A Dutch oven should be stored with its lid ajar to allow the interior to breath and to prevent the lid from becoming adhered to the main body of the oven. A folded sheet of paper towel placed between the lid and the oven will serve the purpose.

- Vegetable oil as a coating agent is the right choice for regular cast iron use. But when storing cast iron for long periods of time, it is better to coat the cast iron in a food-grade mineral oil before storage. Vegetable oils can become gummy or rancid over long periods of storage, especially in warm conditions, whereas food-grade mineral oil will not. Be certain to only use mineral oil that is labeled food grade and only for long-term storage, not day-to-day use.

Reseasoning Cast Iron

Cast iron's protective coating is called "patina" or "seasoning." This coating is nontoxic. It does not come from man-made chemicals but builds naturally on the iron's surface through the cooking process. When wiped with food-grade oil before each use, the microporosity within the cast iron traps and holds the oil, which then hardens under the heat of cooking into a sterile layer with excellent nonstick properties. With a little care both before and after cooking, your cast iron's patina will retain its durable and slippery nature indefinitely.

Most cast iron comes from the factory preseasoned and ready to use. But while the cast iron metal is virtually indestructible, the patina is not. It can be damaged through improper use, cleaning, or storage. The telltale sign that it's time to reseason your cast iron will be the formation of rust spots or significant loss of natural nonstick properties.

Heavy damage to the patina can occur suddenly when a Dutch oven or skillet is left over very hot flames or coals and the food inside completely dries and burns. Large loss of patina can also happen through improper cleaning using harsh detergents or certain types of metal scrub pads. But it can also occur insidiously over time if the cast iron's surface isn't reoiled before and after each meal.

If you find that your cast iron's patina is in bad shape, don't be alarmed! The beauty of patina is that it can be easily repaired. *You should never discard cast iron simply because patina is missing or damaged.* The process of reseasoning cast iron is straightforward and involves little more than baking a layer of cooking oil onto the surface of the metal in a hot grill or kitchen oven. The following steps take you through the process:

1. Use a pad of steel wool to remove rust spots and damaged regions of patina. Scrub the entire surface of the cookware if the situation warrants it. When reseasoning, err on the side of removing too much patina. The new seasoned surface will be more uniform in strength and appearance as a result.

2. Thoroughly wash your cookware, completely dry with a towel, then allow to air-dry for an additional hour or two. The surface must be free of all moisture before the next step.

3. Wipe a heavy layer of vegetable oil or melted shortening over the *entire* surface of the cast iron, both inside and out. Don't forget to do the same with the lid if you're reseasoning a Dutch oven.

4. Place the cookware upside down on the rack of a barbecue grill or kitchen oven. Tilt the base of the Dutch oven or skillet, propping it at an angle on a heat-safe utensil. If a camp Dutch oven, lean the lid against the base, the flanged top facing downward. Excess oil forms sticky patches wherever it pools on the surface. By leaning your cast iron, excess oil will drain from the surface. If using a kitchen oven, place a large sheet of aluminum foil on a rack under the cast iron to catch dripping oil.

5. Close the kitchen oven door or grill lid and bring to medium heat, about 350°F to 400°F. The oil will smoke slightly and, for some, may smell disagreeable. This is normal and shouldn't be a problem when using a grill outdoors. But smoke and odor can be an issue in the home kitchen, especially if a smoke alarm is in the vicinity. In this case, the grill might be a better option.

6. Bake the cast iron for at least one hour. Smoking will probably have abated by then. If not, continue to bake until no more smoke is seen.

7. Allow the cast iron to cool completely before removing from the oven or grill.

8. Your cookware's new seasoned coating may be shiny dark brown instead of black. This is especially true for cast iron seasoned for the first time. The brownish color has no bearing on nonstick performance and will eventually toughen with use into a deep black.

If your new cast iron arrives from the factory bare naked, a gunmetal gray, it will require seasoning before first use. Just follow the directions above, and don't neglect step one: the metal may appear to not need scrubbing, but unseasoned cast iron usually has an invisible waxlike coating applied to prevent rusting on the way from the factory. Use hot water and a thorough scrubbing with a stiff metal pad or brush to remove this coating before moving on to step two.

Breakfast

BAKED EGGS IN AVOCADOS

Total servings: 4
Preparation time: 45 minutes
Challenge level: Easy

V-LO

2 extra-large avocados

4 small eggs

"Everything"-style bagel seasoning to taste

Required equipment:
10-inch camp Dutch oven

Preparation at camp:

1. Prepare 23 coals for the Dutch oven.
2. Slice avocados in half lengthwise.
3. Using a spoon, carefully scoop the seed from each avocado, then remove a little extra avocado flesh to make room for the eggs. You'll have 4 halves total.
4. Line the avocados side-by-side in the oven. Positioning them side-to-side will help stabilize them.
5. Carefully crack a whole egg into each of the 4 depressions left by the seeds.
6. Using 16 coals on the lid and 7 coals under the oven, bake for 25 minutes or until egg whites have set and yolks are cooked to taste.
7. Sprinkle with bagel seasoning and serve.

Christine and Tim Conners
Tucson, Arizona

CAST IRON QUICHE

Total servings: 4 to 6
Preparation time: 1 hour 15 minutes
Challenge level: Moderate

V-LO

Preparation at camp:

1. Preheat Dutch oven using 16 coals on the lid and 7 coals under the oven.
2. Place piecrust, still in its foil pan, in Dutch oven. Return lid to the oven and bake for 12 minutes.
3. Meanwhile, in a large bowl, whisk eggs with the spinach, salt, black pepper, milk, onions, cheese, and optional ham.
4. After the piecrust has finished baking, carefully pour egg mixture into the pie pan, which should still be sitting in the Dutch oven.
5. Return lid to oven and continue to bake for an additional 45 minutes or until the center of the quiche is set. Refresh coals as needed.

Tip:
½ cup of diced ham is about 3 ounces by weight.

Christine and Tim Conners
Tucson, Arizona

1 premade frozen piecrust in pan

5 eggs

1 (10-ounce) package chopped frozen spinach, thawed and drained

¼ teaspoon salt

¼ teaspoon ground black pepper

½ cup whole milk

2 green onions, chopped

¾ cup shredded Swiss cheese

Optional: ½ cup diced cooked ham

Required equipment:
10-inch camp Dutch oven
Large mixing bowl

TWICE-BAKED BREAKFAST POTATOES

V-LO

Total servings: 4
Preparation time: 1 hour (plus preparation time the night before)
Challenge level: Difficult

4 extra-large russet potatoes, washed

1 tablespoon olive oil

5 eggs

Salt and black pepper to taste

1 (4-ounce) container crumbled feta cheese

Optional: crumbled bacon, sausage, or ham

Paprika to taste

Preparation at camp:

1. The night before preparing these for breakfast, coat potatoes in olive oil, poke each aggressively in many places with a fork, then wrap each in heavy-duty aluminum foil.

2. Bake potatoes in the evening campfire. See tips below.

3. Leave foil on the baked potatoes and set them aside in a cool location.

4. In the morning, prepare 21 coals for the Dutch oven.

5. Remove about ¼ of the potato *lengthwise*. Discard or eat this portion from each potato.

6. Being careful to not damage the skin, carefully remove the inside from each potato using a spoon, placing the extracted potato aside in a small bowl. Leave a lining of potato about ¼ inch thick along the skin. Each potato should now be hollowed out.

7. Mash extracted potato with a fork in the small bowl, then crack in the contents of one egg. Mix with the fork, adding salt and black pepper.

8. Add cheese to the inside of each potato, dividing evenly.

9. Crack an egg into each potato.

10. Add optional bacon, sausage, or ham to each potato.

11. Scoop the mashed potato mix back into each potato, dividing equally. The mashed potatoes will form a mound.

12. Sprinkle the potato mix with paprika.

13. Make loosely crumpled balls from the aluminum foil that the potatoes were baked in to hold the potatoes upright in the Dutch oven. The potatoes can also be leaned against the inside wall of the oven for stability.

14. Bake using 14 coals on top of the oven and 7 under the oven for about 30 minutes or until the eggs are cooked to your liking. Refresh coals as needed.

Options:
Substitute a favorite crumbly cheese for the feta, such as gorgonzola, blue cheese, or cotija.

Tips:
Baking potatoes in a campfire is not an exact science and requires attention and patience. Avoid placing the potatoes in the very hot core of the campfire or in the middle of roaring flames. Set potatoes on top of the embers, not buried in them. Turn potatoes every few minutes. After about 30 minutes, begin checking potatoes for tenderness by pinching while using barbecue gloves to avoid burning your fingers. Once potatoes have softened, they can be removed from the fire.

If a campfire isn't available, potatoes can be baked in the Dutch oven at about 400°F (see coal conversion chart at the front of the book).

Ken Spiegel
Medford, New York

Required equipment:
10-inch camp Dutch oven
Heavy-duty aluminum foil

SAUSAGE-CHEESE PULL-APARTS

Total servings: 6 to 8
Preparation time: 45 minutes
Challenge level: Easy

1 (16.3-ounce) container Pillsbury Grands! Flaky Layers Original biscuits

6 eggs

¼ cup whole milk

1 pound precooked sausage

1 cup shredded cheddar cheese

¼ cup finely chopped green onions

Required equipment:
12-inch camp Dutch oven

Preparation at camp:
1. Preheat well-greased Dutch oven over 25 coals.
2. Cut each biscuit into quarters.
3. In a large bowl, beat eggs and milk until smooth.
4. Add sausage, cheese, and onions to the egg mixture. Stir until sausage is crumbled and evenly coated.
5. Spoon sausage mixture into Dutch oven and spread evenly across bottom.
6. Arrange biscuit pieces in a single layer over the sausage mixture.
7. Cover oven. Bake for 25 minutes using 17 coals on the lid and 8 coals under the oven or until biscuits are a light golden brown.

Option:
Goes great with leftover sausage gravy!

Robert "Cowboy Bob" Dowdy
Great Falls, Montana

APPLE VALLEY FRENCH TOAST

Total servings: 6 to 8
Preparation time: 1 hour 30 minutes
Challenge level: Moderate

Preparation at camp:

1. In Dutch oven heated over 21 coals, brown sausage until meat is no longer pink. Remove sausage and set aside.
2. Add sliced apples to the hot oven, then cover and cook for 3 to 5 minutes, until tender. Remove apples and set aside.
3. In a large bowl, whisk eggs, milk, syrup, and nutmeg until combined.
4. Dip about half of the bread slices in the egg mixture, fully coating each, then arrange on the bottom of the oven.
5. Evenly cover bread at the bottom of the oven with the browned sausage, followed by the cooked apples, and finally with the remaining bread slices, also thoroughly dipped in the egg mix.
6. Pour any remaining egg mixture over the top.
7. Bake for 45 minutes using 14 coals on the lid and 7 briquettes under the oven, until the bread is lightly browned. Refresh coals as needed.

Delano LaGow
Oswego, Illinois

1 pound ground turkey sausage

3 medium-size Granny Smith apples, cored, peeled, and cut into slices ½ inch thick

6 eggs

¾ cup whole milk

½ cup maple syrup

½ teaspoon ground nutmeg

½ loaf French bread, sliced ½ inch thick

Required equipment:
10-inch camp Dutch oven
Large mixing bowl

APPLE PAN DOWDY

V-LO

Total servings: 8
Preparation time: 45 minutes
Challenge level: Easy

This is an actual recipe from an 1800s trail-drive reenactment I participated in. It is very easy to prepare and a great way to use leftover biscuits. PS: Don't forget the coffee!

8 fully cooked biscuits

1 tablespoon butter, softened

3 Granny Smith apples, skin on and cored

⅔ cup granulated sugar

1 teaspoon ground cinnamon

¼ teaspoon ground nutmeg

¼ teaspoon salt

½ cup water

Required equipment:
12-inch camp Dutch oven
Heavy-duty aluminum foil

Preparation at camp:

1. Prepare 25 coals for the Dutch oven.
2. Evenly distribute biscuits over the bottom of a Dutch oven lined with heavy-duty aluminum foil.
3. Spread butter over tops of the biscuits.
4. Cut apples into slices about ¼ inch thick. Lay apple slices over the biscuits.
5. Sprinkle sugar, cinnamon, nutmeg, and salt over the apples.
6. Pour water between the biscuits into the bottom of the oven.
7. Bake using 17 coals on the lid and 8 coals under the oven for about 25 minutes or until the apples are cooked through.

Tip:
The biscuits for this recipe must be precooked, either store-bought that way (not always readily available), leftovers from a previous breakfast, or baked in the Dutch oven just prior to use in this recipe. It is quick and easy to bake a batch of store-bought biscuit dough.

Robert "Cowboy Bob" Dowdy
Great Falls, Montana

BREAKFAST STICKY BUNS

V-LO

Total servings: 8
Preparation time: 45 minutes
Challenge level: Easy

Preparation at camp:
1. Prepare 23 coals for the Dutch oven.
2. Stir butter and syrup together in a small bowl and set aside.
3. In a second small bowl, combine sugar, cinnamon, and optional nuts.
4. Line Dutch oven with heavy-duty aluminum foil.
5. Spread about half of the butter mixture over the foil in the bottom of the oven, then sprinkle about half of the sugar mixture over the butter mixture.
6. Cut each biscuit into quarters and evenly arrange the pieces over the bottom of the oven.
7. Spread the remaining butter mixture over the biscuits and sprinkle the remaining sugar mixture over the top.
8. Bake using 16 coals on the lid and 7 coals under the oven for about 25 minutes or until the biscuits have risen and are a light golden brown.
9. Allow biscuits to cool for a few minutes, then carefully lift the biscuits from the oven using the foil and invert onto a tray or large plate.

Robert "Cowboy Bob" Dowdy
Great Falls, Montana

3 tablespoons butter, softened

½ cup maple syrup

⅓ cup packed brown sugar

½ teaspoon ground cinnamon

Optional: ¾ cup chopped pecans

1 (16.3-ounce) container Pillsbury Grands! Southern Homestyle Buttermilk biscuits

Required equipment:
10-inch camp Dutch oven
2 small mixing bowls
Heavy-duty aluminum foil

COWBOY BOB'S BISCUITS AND GRAVY

Total servings: 8
Preparation time: 1 hour 15 minutes
Challenge level: Moderate

My dad made the best gravy in the South. My sisters and I fight over who makes the best gravy now!

Gravy:

½ pound ground pork sausage

2 tablespoons butter

¼ cup all-purpose flour

3 cups whole milk

¼ teaspoon seasoned salt

½ teaspoon salt

1 teaspoon ground black pepper

1 dash hot sauce (your favorite)

¼ teaspoon granulated sugar

Biscuits:

2 cups all-purpose flour plus extra to work dough

1 tablespoon granulated sugar

½ teaspoon baking soda

2 teaspoons baking powder

¾ teaspoon salt

1 cup buttermilk

½ cup (1 standard stick) butter, softened

Preparation at camp:

To prepare gravy:

1. Brown sausage in Dutch oven over 33 coals until sausage is no longer pink.
2. Add butter and stir until melted.
3. Sprinkle flour into oven and stir continuously for about 2 minutes.
4. Slowly pour milk into oven, using a whisk to constantly stir the mixture to avoid clumping.
5. Using the whisk, blend in seasoned salt, salt, pepper, hot sauce, and sugar. Taste gravy and adjust seasonings if desired.
6. Remove oven from coals.
7. Allow gravy to cool for a few minutes before carefully pouring into a medium-size bowl.
8. Wipe remaining gravy from the bottom and sides of oven and set the oven aside.

To prepare biscuits:

1. Mix together 2 cups of flour, sugar, baking soda, baking powder, and salt in a large bowl.
2. In a medium-size bowl, stir together the buttermilk and softened butter.
3. Pour buttermilk mixture into the large bowl containing the flour mixture. Combine all ingredients to make a stiff dough.
4. Sprinkle flour over a large cutting board and lay down the dough ball on the board, covering the ball with a sprinkle of flour. Using clean hands, knead the ball well.
5. Using a rolling pin, roll the dough flat until about ¾ inch thick.

6. With a biscuit cutter, punch out 8 biscuits from the sheet of dough and evenly arrange the biscuits, flat side down, in the bottom of the Dutch oven. The remaining dough can be discarded or rolled into small balls and set between the biscuits in the oven.
7. Set lid on oven and move 22 coals to the lid and 11 coals under the oven. Refresh coals if necessary.
8. Bake for about 20 minutes or until biscuits have risen and are a light golden brown.
9. Serve biscuits covered in gravy.

Required equipment:
12-inch camp Dutch oven
Whisk
2 medium-size mixing bowls
Large mixing bowl
Large cutting board
Rolling pin
Biscuit cutter

Option:
Sour cream can be stirred into the gravy mix after cooking the gravy to make it extra creamy. Consider experimenting with sour cream, using a small amount for your first batch and increasing as desired from there.

Tips:
A cylindrical water bottle can be used to roll the dough if a rolling pin is not available. In addition, a clean, empty metal can can be used as a biscuit cutter.

Robert "Cowboy Bob" Dowdy
Great Falls, Montana

DANG GOOD DONUTS

Total servings: 8
Preparation time: 45 minutes
Challenge level: Difficult

V-LO

4 cups sunflower oil

1 (16-ounce) container refrigerated biscuit dough

1 cup powdered sugar

Optional toppings: cinnamon sugar, honey, honey butter, melted chocolate

Required equipment:
10-inch camp Dutch oven
Cooking thermometer
Empty plastic soda bottle
Paper towels
Paper lunch bags

Preparation at camp:

1. Pour oil in Dutch oven and set over 21 coals. Warm the oil until it reaches 350°F, using a cooking thermometer to measure temperature. The oil should be hot enough to quickly fry the donuts, but not so hot that the donuts turn dark brown before cooking through. If the oil is becoming too hot, carefully remove some of the coals from under the oven to bring the temperature down.

2. While the oil is heating, open the biscuit dough container, separate the biscuits, and place on a clean surface.

3. Grease the top of an empty, clean plastic soda bottle with a little of the unheated oil. Use the bottle to punch holes in the center of each of the biscuits by pressing the opening into the dough. The residual dough should slide from the bottle opening.

4. Place the donuts into hot oil, being careful to avoid splattering. Do not overload your oven; you'll have better results by cooking a few at a time rather than all at once. Don't forget to cook the donut "holes" also!

5. Once the donuts become a golden brown, remove from oil and place on paper towels to draw off excess grease.

6. Fill a few paper lunch bags with the powdered sugar.

7. Carefully place a drained donut into a paper bag and shake to coat. Repeat for each of the remaining donuts.

8. Eat as is or with your favorite topping.

Bill Britt
Hurlburt Field, Florida

44

APPLE CRUMBLE COFFEE CAKE

Total servings: 8 to 10
Preparation time: 1 hour 15 minutes
Challenge level: Moderate

V-LO

Another nod to the great orchardist Johnny Appleseed, whose wisdom assured we'd have plenty of fruit with which to make this coffee cake packed with tasty goodness!

Preparation at camp:

1. Prepare 25 coals for the Dutch oven.
2. To prepare cake batter, mix all dry cake ingredients in a large bowl.
3. Add eggs, vanilla extract, butter, and sour cream to the bowl. Stir well.
4. Fold sliced apples into batter.
5. Line Dutch oven with heavy-duty aluminum foil, then pour cake batter into oven.
6. Add all topping ingredients to a medium-sized bowl and mix together.
7. Sprinkle topping over cake batter.
8. Using 17 coals on the lid and 8 coals under the oven, bake for about 45 minutes, rotating oven and lid a quarter turn in opposite directions every 15 minutes or so until a toothpick or knife inserted in the center of the cake comes out clean. Refresh coals as needed.

Ken Shelby
Grandview, Missouri

Cake:
2 cups all-purpose flour
1 teaspoon baking soda
1 teaspoon ground cinnamon
1½ cups packed brown sugar
½ teaspoon salt
2 large eggs
1 teaspoon vanilla extract
½ cup (1 standard stick) butter, softened
1 cup sour cream
2 apples, peeled, cored, and thinly sliced

Crumble topping:
½ cup all-purpose flour
½ cup packed brown sugar
½ teaspoon ground cinnamon
¼ cup (½ standard stick) butter, softened

Required equipment:
12-inch camp Dutch oven
Large mixing bowl
Medium-size mixing bowl
Heavy-duty aluminum foil
Toothpick or knife

SONORAN SCRAMBLE

V-LO

Total servings: 2
Preparation time: 20 minutes
Challenge level: Easy

1 tablespoon butter

4 eggs

¼ cup salsa

2 tablespoons sour cream

Salt and black pepper to taste

1 avocado, sliced

Required equipment:
Medium-size skillet

Preparation at camp:

1. Melt butter in skillet over medium heat.
2. Crack eggs into skillet, then add salsa, sour cream, salt, and black pepper.
3. Mix ingredients together and scramble continuously with a spatula until eggs congeal to desired consistency.
4. Serve, topping with sliced avocado.

Christine and Tim Conners
Tucson, Arizona

AVOCADO BREAKFAST TOAST

Total servings: 2
Preparation time: 20 minutes
Challenge level: Easy

V

Preparation at camp:

1. In a skillet over medium heat, warm the olive oil.
2. Toast both sides of bread in skillet, then set on a plate.
3. In a bowl, combine avocado, salt, and garlic. Mash with a fork until garlic is uniformly distributed.
4. Place basil leaves over the face of each slice of toast.
5. Divide avocado mixture over the face of each slice, covering the basil leaves.
6. Drizzle with balsamic vinegar glaze.

Tip:
For this recipe, look for balsamic vinegar that has a thick consistency.

Christine and Tim Conners
Tucson, Arizona

1 tablespoon olive oil

2 slices hearty whole-grain bread

1 large avocado, sliced

⅛ teaspoon salt

2 cloves garlic, pressed

6 basil leaves

1 teaspoon balsamic vinegar glaze, to taste

Required equipment:
Medium-size skillet
Medium-size mixing bowl

SMOKED SALMON AND AVOCADO TOAST

Total servings: 2
Preparation time: 20 minutes
Challenge level: Easy

2 tablespoons olive oil

4 slices whole-grain artisan bread

4 ounces smoked salmon

1 large avocado, sliced

1 lemon, cut into quarters

Fresh dill weed to taste

Salt and black pepper to taste

Optional: ½ cup cottage cheese

Required equipment:
Medium-size skillet

Preparation at camp:
1. Warm oil in a skillet over medium heat.
2. Toast both sides of bread in skillet, then set on a plate.
3. Divide salmon and avocado slices over toast.
4. Sprinkle lemon juice and fresh dill weed over salmon and avocado slices. Add salt and black pepper to taste.
5. Serve with optional cottage cheese.

Options:
Substitute pumpernickel or rye for the artisan bread.

Christine and Tim Conners
Tucson, Arizona

ZUGSPITZE EGGS BENEDICT

Total servings: 2
Preparation time: 45 minutes
Challenge level: Moderate

Preparation at camp:

1. In a dry skillet over medium heat, toast the English muffin halves. Don't let them burn. Set muffins aside.
2. Melt butter in a pot. Do not overcook.
3. Remove pot from heat and add lemon juice and egg yolk. Stir.
4. Return pot to medium heat, stirring constantly until thick. Don't allow the mixture to curdle.
5. Add sour cream, stir, then heat for an additional minute. Avoid boiling; this would cause the sauce to separate.
6. Add salt and black pepper to taste, then set hollandaise sauce aside.
7. In the same skillet used to toast the bread, warm oil over medium heat and fry bacon on both sides. Set bacon aside.
8. Fry eggs, either sunny-side up or over easy, in the skillet. Salt and pepper the eggs to taste.
9. Place half of a toasted muffin, cut-side up, on separate serving plates. Top each muffin with one slice of fried bacon and one fried egg, then divide hollandaise sauce equally over each.

Charles Bostick
Munich, Germany

2 English muffins, halved

2 tablespoons butter

1 tablespoon fresh lemon juice

1 egg yolk (for hollandaise sauce)

½ cup sour cream

Salt and black pepper to taste

1 tablespoon olive oil

4 slices Canadian bacon, thick sliced

4 eggs (for muffins)

Required equipment:
Large skillet
Small cook pot

CREPES OF THE PYRENEES

Total servings: 2 to 4
Preparation time: 45 minutes
Challenge level: Moderate

Crepes can be served sweet or savory. Choose your favorite fillings to fit your style!

1 cup whole milk

4 eggs

¼ teaspoon salt

1 cup all-purpose flour

¼ cup (½ standard stick) butter

Savory fillings: fresh spinach, basil, exotic cheeses, cream, cooked sliced mushrooms, pesto, smoked salmon, cooked ham, cooked sausage, grilled vegetables, onions

Sweet fillings: cream cheese, powdered sugar, ground cinnamon, Nutella, fresh or canned fruit, fruit preserves, whipped cream, chopped nuts, mini marshmallows, chocolate chips, Greek yogurt, lemon curd, pie filling

Required equipment:
Small skillet
Large mixing bowl
Whisk

Preparation at camp:

1. Combine milk, eggs, and salt in a bowl. Whisk into a smooth liquid.
2. Slowly add flour to the bowl. Whisk briskly to ensure the batter remains very thin with no clumps.
3. Heat a small skillet over medium-high heat.
4. Melt about 1 tablespoon butter to coat the pan.
5. Pour about ½ cup crepe batter into pan, enough to just cover the pan as the batter is swirled around in the skillet.
6. Once the top of the crepe is dry, use a spatula to carefully loosen the crepe and flip the crepe over.
7. Cook for just a few moments before transferring crepe to a plate.
8. Evenly top crepe with your favorite fillings and roll into a log.
9. Repeat steps 4 through 8 for the remaining batter.

Mike "Mountain Man Mike" Lancaster
Clovis, California

SMOKED SALMON SCRAMBLED EGGS

Total servings: 3 to 4
Preparation time: 30 minutes
Challenge level: Easy

Preparation at camp:

1. Using a fork, mix eggs in a bowl.
2. Remove skin from salmon, then shred salmon into pieces.
3. Add shredded salmon, sour cream, onions, and tomatoes to the eggs and mix well.
4. Melt butter in skillet over medium heat.
5. Pour egg mixture into pan, continuously scrambling with a spatula until eggs congeal and reach desired consistency.
6. Remove scrambled eggs from heat, then add salt and black pepper to taste.

Christine and Tim Conners
Tucson, Arizona

6 eggs

4 ounces smoked salmon

¼ cup sour cream

2 green onions, chopped

6 grape tomatoes, sliced into quarters

1 tablespoon butter

Salt and black pepper to taste

Required equipment:
Medium-size skillet
Large mixing bowl

PINNACLE PANCAKES

V-LO

Total servings: 3 to 4
Preparation time: 30 minutes
Challenge level: Moderate

1 cup all-purpose flour

2 tablespoons granulated sugar

2 teaspoons baking powder

⅛ teaspoon salt

1 cup whole milk

1 egg

¼ cup (½ standard stick) butter

Maple syrup to taste

Required equipment:
Medium-size skillet
Large mixing bowl

Preparation at camp:

1. Combine flour, sugar, baking powder, salt, milk, and egg in a large bowl.
2. Stir batter well until all large clumps are gone.
3. Melt butter in skillet over medium heat. Use about 1 tablespoon of butter for each pancake.
4. Working in batches, pour some of the batter into pan, cooking one or two pancakes at a time. Do not try to use all of the batter at once!
5. Once top of pancake begins to bubble, flip and brown the other side. Pay close attention here because the second side will brown much more quickly than the first!
6. Serve pancakes with maple syrup.

Christine and Tim Conners
Tucson, Arizona

BREAKFAST IN THE DUNES

Total servings: 4 to 6
Preparation time: 45 minutes
Challenge level: Easy

V-LO

Preparation at camp:
1. In a bowl, whisk eggs with mustard and salt.
2. Melt butter in skillet over medium heat.
3. Add onion and garlic to skillet. Sauté until onion caramelizes.
4. Add bread cubes to skillet and toss, allowing edges of the bread cubes to toast slightly.
5. Pour egg mixture over bread in skillet and gently stir until eggs congeal and are cooked through.
6. Add cheese, stir, and serve.

Tip:
One tablespoon pressed garlic is equal to about 6 cloves.

Christine and Tim Conners
Tucson, Arizona

6 eggs

1 tablespoon Dijon mustard

¼ teaspoon salt

2 tablespoons butter

1 sweet onion, diced

1 tablespoon pressed garlic

½ loaf sourdough bread (about 8 ounces), cubed

1 cup shredded Swiss cheese

Required equipment:
Medium-size skillet
Medium-size mixing bowl

CAVEMAN BREAKFAST

Total servings: 4 to 6
Preparation time: 45 minutes
Challenge level: Easy

1 pound ground pork

2 teaspoons ground sage

1 teaspoon garlic powder

1 teaspoon ground fennel

½ teaspoon ground coriander

Salt and black pepper to taste

Maple syrup to taste

1 (10-ounce) package frozen butternut squash chunks, thawed

Required equipment:
Medium-size skillet

Preparation at camp:
1. Brown meat in a skillet over medium heat.
2. Stir in spices, salt, black pepper, and maple syrup.
3. Add squash, stir well, and reduce heat to low.
4. Cook while occasionally stirring for 30 minutes or until squash is fork-tender.

Jim "Cinnamonboy" Rausch
Ellsworth, Maine

OMELET PRIMAVERA

V-LO

Total servings: 4 to 6
Preparation time: 1 hour
Challenge level: Moderate

Preparation at camp:

1. Whisk eggs in a large bowl.
2. Combine tomatoes, corn, and zucchini in a small, lightly oiled skillet over medium heat. Fry vegetables until zucchini is soft.
3. Set vegetable mix aside in a small bowl, then cover vegetables with the cheese.
4. Carefully wipe the skillet and add 1 tablespoon of oil. Spread oil over surface of pan.
5. Pour half of the whisked eggs into the skillet, then cover with lid or sheet of foil. Occasionally shake the pan gently to help the eggs cook evenly.
6. Once eggs fully congeal, gently loosen eggs from pan with a spatula, then carefully slide eggs onto a large plate.
7. Cover half of the omelet with half of the vegetable-cheese mixture. Fold the half of the omelet not covered with vegetables over the half that is.
8. Top the omelet with half of the avocado slices and sprinkle cilantro to taste over the avocado. Add salt and black pepper to taste.
9. Repeat steps 4 through 8 for the second omelet using remaining ingredients.

Christine and Tim Conners
Tucson, Arizona

8 eggs

2 tablespoons olive oil, plus small amount to fry vegetables

8 ounces sun-dried tomatoes in oil and herbs, drained and chopped

1 (8.5-ounce) can corn, drained

1 small zucchini, diced

4 ounces shredded Gruyere cheese

1 avocado, sliced

1 small bunch fresh cilantro, stemmed and chopped

Salt and black pepper to taste

Required equipment:
Small skillet
Large mixing bowl
Small mixing bowl

CAMP MATAGUAY GARLIC FRENCH TOAST

Total servings: 4 to 8
Preparation time: 1 hour
Challenge level: Moderate

Dedicated to a memorable, raccoon-filled summer at Mataguay Boy Scout Camp!

8 slices bacon

8 eggs

¾ cup whole milk

3 cloves garlic, minced

¼ cup finely minced parsley leaves

Salt and black pepper to taste

1 cup grated Parmesan cheese

2 tablespoons butter

8 slices French bread

Maple syrup to taste

Required equipment:
Large skillet
Large mixing bowl

Preparation at camp:
1. Cook bacon in skillet over medium heat, then set aside. Drain skillet.
2. Fry 4 eggs, sunny-side up (i.e., don't flip). Set eggs aside, being careful to not burst the yolks.
3. In a large bowl, whisk together 4 eggs, milk, garlic, parsley, salt, and black pepper.
4. Pour Parmesan cheese evenly over a large plate.
5. Once it has cooled to the touch, wipe the skillet.
6. Melt butter in skillet over medium heat.
7. Dip bread slices in egg mixture, then dredge in Parmesan cheese, coating both sides well.
8. Lay coated bread slices in skillet and fry both sides to a golden brown. Repeat until all toast is cooked.
9. Assemble the cooked slices of French toast like a sandwich, adding 2 pieces of bacon and 1 egg to each.
10. Place the sandwiches on a plate, cutting each in half, and serve with maple syrup.

Tip:
Use a sheet of foil over the skillet while the eggs are frying to help speed the cooking process.

Paul Krebs
Carlsbad, California

BAJA BREAKFAST BURRITOS

Total servings: 6
Preparation time: 45 minutes
Challenge level: Easy

Preparation at camp:

1. Warm oil in skillet over medium heat.
2. Fry chorizo until fully cooked.
3. Add eggs and onion to the skillet and scramble until eggs congeal.
4. Evenly divide egg mixture, queso, tomatoes, cilantro, and avocado slices among the 6 tortillas.
5. Roll tortillas, tucking in the corners.
6. Can be eaten as is or heated briefly first in a clean skillet beginning with the seam-side down.

Christine and Tim Conners
Tucson, Arizona

1 tablespoon vegetable oil

12 ounces chorizo

6 eggs, beaten

1 small onion, chopped

1 cup crumbled queso fresco

1 pint cherry tomatoes, sliced into quarters

1 bunch fresh cilantro, stemmed and chopped

2 large avocados, sliced

6 large flour tortillas

Required equipment:
Large skillet

WILD BERRY PANCAKES

V-LO

Total servings: 6 to 8
Preparation time: 45 minutes
Challenge level: Moderate

2 cups all-purpose flour

¼ cup granulated sugar

1 tablespoon baking powder

¼ teaspoon salt

2 eggs

2 cups whole milk

1 cup fresh berries (your choice)

1 tablespoon butter

Toppings: maple syrup, powdered sugar, whipped cream

Required equipment:
Medium-size skillet
Medium-size mixing bowl

Preparation at camp:

1. In a bowl, mix together flour, sugar, baking powder, and salt.
2. Add eggs and milk. Stir well, then carefully fold in the berries.
3. Warm butter in skillet over medium heat.
4. Pour about ½ cup of batter into skillet. When top of pancake begins to bubble, flip and brown the other side. Pay close attention here because the second side will brown much more quickly than the first!
5. Repeat step 4 until all the batter is used.
6. Serve with favorite toppings.

*Christine and Tim Conners
Tucson, Arizona*

FREE SPIRIT FRENCH TOAST

V-LO

Total servings: 6 to 8
Preparation time: 45 minutes
Challenge level: Moderate

Preparation at camp:
1. Crack eggs into a large bowl and whisk.
2. Add half-and-half and vanilla to the bowl and whisk well.
3. Cut bread into slices about ½ to 1 inch thick.
4. Melt 1 tablespoon of butter in a skillet over medium heat.
5. Dip slices of bread into egg mixture and submerge so that both sides are coated.
6. Place slices of coated bread into skillet. Don't crowd the skillet.
7. Cook both sides until golden brown.
8. Move cooked French toast to a serving tray.
9. Repeat steps 4 through 8 until all bread has been cooked.
10. Serve with your favorite toppings.

Christine and Tim Conners
Tucson, Arizona

6 eggs

1 cup half-and-half

¼ teaspoon vanilla extract

½ loaf French bread

¼ cup (½ standard stick) butter

Toppings: confectioner's sugar, maple syrup, whipped cream

Required equipment:
Large skillet
Large mixing bowl

GRUMPY'S STUFFED FRENCH TOAST

Total servings: 8 to 10
Preparation time: 45 minutes
Challenge level: Moderate

V-LO

Decadent and delicious!

1 (8-ounce) package cream cheese, softened

1½ teaspoons vanilla extract

½ cup chopped walnuts

4 eggs

1 cup heavy whipping cream

½ teaspoon ground nutmeg

1 loaf "Texas toast"–style bread, sliced

1 (12-ounce) jar apricot preserves

½ cup orange juice

Required equipment:
Large skillet
Small mixing bowl
Medium-size mixing bowl
Small cook pot

Preparation at camp:

1. Beat together cream cheese and 1 teaspoon vanilla extract in a small bowl, then stir in the walnuts.

2. In a medium-size bowl, mix together eggs, heavy cream, ½ teaspoon vanilla extract, and ground nutmeg.

3. Spread a heaping tablespoon of cream cheese mixture between two slices of bread and close like a sandwich. Repeat until all the bread along with all the cream cheese mixture is used up.

4. Heavily oil the skillet and warm it over medium heat.

5. Dip each of the "sandwiches" into the egg mixture to fully coat, then fry on both sides until golden brown. Don't crowd the pan; cook in batches instead.

6. While French toast is frying, warm preserves and orange juice stirred together in a small pot over low heat.

7. Once all the toast is finished cooking, drizzle the warm preserve mixture over the slices before serving.

Michael "Grumpy" Wyatt
Noblesville, Indiana

OATMEAL IN BULK

Total servings: 16
Preparation time: 10 minutes
Challenge level: Easy

V-LO

Preparation at home:
1. In a large container, combine oats, granolas, muesli, seeds, and chocolate.
2. Seal well, shake to mix, and keep cool until ready to use.

Preparation at camp:
1. To prepare 1 serving, combine 1 cup dried oatmeal mix with 1 cup milk in a small skillet.
2. Heat until simmering, stirring occasionally.
3. Remove from heat and serve with optional honey or fresh berries.

Ken Spiegel
Medford, New York

1 (18-ounce) container old-fashioned oats

1 (11-ounce) package Nature Valley Cranberry-Almond granola

1 (11-ounce) package Nature Valley Oats and Honey granola

1 (18-ounce) package Bob's Red Mill Old Country Style muesli

1 cup raw pepitas

1 cup sunflower seed kernels

1 (3.5-ounce) bar dark chocolate, chopped into small bits

1 cup whole milk

Optional: honey or fresh berries

Required equipment:
Small skillet

PIE IRON MEXICAN OMELET

V-LO

Total servings: 1
Preparation time: 20 minutes
Challenge level: Moderate

1 teaspoon butter, softened

1 egg

1 tablespoon pico de gallo

2 tablespoons Mexican blend shredded cheese

Salt and black pepper to taste

Salsa and fresh chopped cilantro to taste

Required equipment:
Pie iron
Small mixing bowl

Preparation at camp:

1. Coat inside of the pie iron with butter.
2. In a bowl, whisk together egg, pico de gallo, cheese, salt, and black pepper.
3. Carefully pour egg mixture into one side of the pie iron.
4. Seal iron and cook for about 5 minutes on each side over the heat of a campfire or grill. Do not hold the pie iron directly in the flame for an extended length of time or the egg mixture may burn.
5. Remove iron from heat, open the iron, and very carefully remove the omelet.
6. Cover omelet in salsa and cilantro to taste.

Tip:
This recipe is appropriate for a pie iron roughly 4 by 4 inches square. For a pie iron of different size, scale the ingredients accordingly, remembering that precision isn't critical here.

Christine and Tim Conners
Tucson, Arizona

COUNTRY PIE IRON OMELET

Total servings: 1
Preparation time: 20 minutes
Challenge level: Moderate

Preparation at camp:
1. Coat inside of the pie iron with butter.
2. In a bowl, whisk together egg, ham, salt, and black pepper.
3. Carefully pour egg mixture into one side of the pie iron.
4. Lay cheese slice over egg mixture.
5. Seal iron and cook for about 5 minutes on each side over the heat of a campfire or grill. Do not hold the pie iron directly in the flame for an extended length of time or the egg mixture may burn.
6. Remove iron from heat, open the iron, and very carefully remove the omelet.

Options:
Substitute your favorite shredded cheese for the cheddar, or try Spam instead of ham. In addition, a small amount of chopped veggies can be added to the egg mixture when whisking.

Tip:
This recipe is appropriate for a pie iron roughly 4 by 4 inches square. For a pie iron of different size, scale the ingredients accordingly, remembering that precision isn't critical here.

Christine and Tim Conners
Tucson, Arizona

1 teaspoon butter, softened

1 egg

1 ounce canned ham, chopped into small pieces

Salt and black pepper to taste

1 slice cheddar cheese

Required equipment:
Pie iron
Small mixing bowl

HASH BROWN PIE IRON CASSEROLE

Total servings: 1
Preparation time: 20 minutes
Challenge level: Moderate

V-LO

1 teaspoon butter, softened

1 small egg

2 thin patties frozen hash brown potatoes

1 slice cheddar cheese

Salt and black pepper to taste

Required equipment:
Pie iron
Small mixing bowl

Preparation at camp:

1. Coat inside of the pie iron with butter.
2. Whisk egg in a bowl.
3. Break hash browns into pieces that fit within the walls of the pie iron. Add hash brown pieces to both pockets of the iron.
4. Carefully pour whisked egg over hash browns in one side of the iron.
5. Lay cheese slice over hash browns in the other side of the iron.
6. Carefully seal iron and cook for about 5 minutes on each side over the heat of a campfire or grill. Do not hold the pie iron directly in the flame for an extended length of time or the egg may burn.
7. Remove iron from heat, open the iron, and very carefully remove the contents.
8. Add salt and black pepper to taste.

Tip:
This recipe is appropriate for a pie iron roughly 4 by 4 inches square. For a pie iron of different size, scale the ingredients accordingly, remembering that precision isn't critical here.

Christine and Tim Conners
Tucson, Arizona

SCRAMBLED FRENCH TOAST IN A PIE IRON

Total servings: 1
Preparation time: 20 minutes
Challenge level: Moderate

V-LO

Preparation at camp:
1. Coat inside of the pie iron with butter.
2. In a bowl, whisk together egg, maple syrup, cinnamon, and salt.
3. Cut bread slices in small pieces.
4. Blend bread pieces into the egg mixture.
5. Pour coated bread pieces into one side of the pie iron, piling them as necessary to fit.
6. Seal iron and cook for about 5 minutes on each side over the heat of a campfire or grill. Do not hold the pie iron directly in the flame for an extended length of time or the bread and egg mixture may burn.
7. Remove iron from heat, open the iron, and very carefully remove the contents.

Tip:
This recipe is appropriate for a pie iron roughly 4 by 4 inches square. For a pie iron of different size, scale the ingredients accordingly, remembering that precision isn't critical here.

Ken Spiegel
Medford, New York

1 teaspoon butter, softened

1 egg

2 teaspoons maple syrup

½ teaspoon ground cinnamon

1 pinch salt

2 small slices bread

Required equipment:
Pie iron
Small mixing bowl

Lunch

MINUTE PIZZA MINIS

V-LO

Total servings: 2
Preparation time: 45 minutes
Challenge level: Easy

2 short French bread baguettes

½ cup pizza sauce

½ cup shredded mozzarella cheese

Optional toppings: sliced pepperoni, crumbled cooked sausage, chopped onion, sliced bell pepper, pineapple, spinach, sliced mushrooms, sliced olives, garlic, chopped precooked ham, chopped precooked chicken

Required equipment:
10-inch camp Dutch oven

Preparation at camp:

1. Preheat Dutch oven using 14 coals on the lid and 7 coals under the oven.
2. Slice each of the baguettes lengthwise as if cutting them to make a sandwich.
3. Evenly spread pizza sauce over the face of each of the 4 pieces of bread.
4. Add desired optional toppings, then divide the cheese over the toppings.
5. Set pizza minis in the oven. There may be some overlap if your baguettes are on the large side. Trim as needed.
6. Cover oven and bake for 15 minutes or until cheese is melted.

Options:
Pesto, barbecue sauce, or teriyaki sauce can be substituted for the pizza sauce.

Jim "Cinnamonboy" Rausch
Ellsworth, Maine

CIABATTA SANDWICHES

Total servings: 3
Preparation time: 1 hour
Challenge level: Easy

Preparation at camp:
1. Prepare 21 coals for the Dutch oven.
2. Grease oven with oil.
3. Open the ciabatta rolls and add 2 tablespoons of pesto sauce and about ⅓ of the salami and mozzarella cheese to each. Close the rolls.
4. Cut each sandwich in two to make 6 halves.
5. Set sandwich halves side-by-side in the oven.
6. Bake using 14 coals on the lid and 7 coals under the oven for about 30 minutes or until the sandwiches are heated through.
7. Remove sandwiches from oven and add sliced tomato and optional ingredients.

Option:
Add the tomato slices *before* baking!

Tip:
Ciabatta bread is squarish. For this recipe, look for rolls that are about 4 inches on a side.

Ken Spiegel
Medford, New York

1 tablespoon olive oil

3 ciabatta bread rolls

6 tablespoons pesto sauce

3 ounces sliced salami or prosciutto

1 (8-ounce) package regular or marinated fresh mozzarella cheese ball, cut into slices

1 beefsteak tomato, sliced

Optional: fresh basil and sun-dried tomatoes

Required equipment:
10-inch camp Dutch oven

CRABBY STUFFED MUSHROOMS

Total servings: 4
Preparation time: 45 minutes
Challenge level: Easy

4 portobella mushrooms

8 ounces real crabmeat

½ cup shredded
Parmesan cheese

3 tablespoons
mayonnaise

3 green onions, chopped

¼ teaspoon seasoned
salt

¼ cup bread crumbs

1 tablespoon butter,
softened

Required equipment:
10-inch camp Dutch
oven
Medium-size mixing
bowl

Preparation at camp:

1. Prepare 21 coals for the Dutch oven.
2. Rinse mushrooms and pat dry with a paper towel. Remove as much of each stem as possible.
3. Combine crabmeat, cheese, mayonnaise, onions, and seasoned salt in a bowl. Mix well.
4. Set mushrooms top-side down, hollowed side facing upward, and divide the crab mixture evenly among the mushroom hollows.
5. Combine bread crumbs with softened butter in the bowl and stir gently.
6. Evenly divide buttered bread crumbs over the mushrooms.
7. Set mushrooms side-by-side in Dutch oven.
8. Using 14 coals on the lid and 7 coals under the oven, bake for about 25 minutes or until the crabmeat is warmed through.

Option:
Crushed Ritz crackers can be used in place of the bread crumbs.

Christine and Tim Conners
Tucson, Arizona

HAMBURGER PIE

Total servings: 4 to 6
Preparation time: 45 minutes
Challenge level: Easy

Preparation at camp:
1. In Dutch oven over 23 coals, brown the ground beef along with the diced onions until meat is no longer pink.
2. Remove oven from coals, then stir in the tomato sauce.
3. Sprinkle cheese over the meat mixture.
4. Evenly layer the crescent roll dough over the cheese.
5. Place lid on oven and move 16 coals to the top, leaving 7 coals underneath.
6. Bake for about 15 minutes or until dough becomes a light golden brown.

Delano LaGow
Oswego, Illinois

1 pound lean ground beef

1 small onion, diced

1 (8-ounce) can tomato sauce

1 (8-ounce) package shredded cheese (your choice)

1 (8-ounce) container refrigerated crescent rolls

Required equipment:
10-inch camp Dutch oven

JACKED UP NACHOS

Total servings: 6 to 8
Preparation time: 45 minutes
Challenge level: Easy

V-LO

This is an easy lunch to prepare, one that the kids will love! Prepare the basic recipe, then mix and match the options to make it your own.

1 (12-ounce) package restaurant-style tortilla chips

1 (10-ounce) package queso fresco

1 (15-ounce) can black beans, rinsed and drained

1 (6.5-ounce) can sliced black olives, drained

10 ounces pico de gallo

Optional: sliced jalapeños, canned corn, sliced avocados, chopped cilantro, chopped green onions, sour cream, guacamole

Required equipment:
10-inch camp Dutch oven

Preparation at camp:

1. Prepare 21 coals for the Dutch oven.
2. Evenly arrange tortilla chips in oven.
3. Crumble queso fresco all around the chips. Gently toss chips to be sure some of the cheese makes it to the bottom.
4. Cover chips with beans and olives along with any optional ingredients you may want heated.
5. Bake for 30 minutes using 14 coals on the lid and 7 coals under the oven.
6. Toss chips with tongs to evenly distribute ingredients.
7. Serve with pico de gallo and any other optional fresh ingredients.

Christine and Tim Conners
Tucson, Arizona

ROLLING RIVER REUBEN

Total servings: 6
Preparation time: 1 hour
Challenge level: Easy

This easy Dutch oven adaptation of a classic will impress even the most experienced outdoor chefs!

Preparation at camp:

1. Prepare 21 coals for the Dutch oven.
2. Cut rye bread into rectangular pieces about 1 to 2 inches on a side.
3. Slice corned beef into thin strips.
4. In Dutch oven lightly coated with oil, evenly distribute half of the rye bread pieces over bottom of oven.
5. Lay corned beef over the bread pieces, then evenly cover with sauerkraut, dressing, and caraway seed.
6. Cover with the remaining bread pieces, then evenly distribute the Swiss cheese slices over bread. Trim slices of cheese as needed to cover all the bread.
7. Using 14 coals on the lid and 7 coals under the oven, bake for about 35 minutes.

Option:
Pastrami can be substituted for the corned beef.

*Christine and Tim Conners
Tucson, Arizona*

6 slices rye bread

1 pound deli-sliced corned beef

1 (14.5-ounce) can sauerkraut

¾ cup Thousand Island dressing

1 tablespoon caraway seed

8 ounces sliced Swiss cheese

Required equipment:
10-inch camp Dutch oven

CHICKEN ALFREDO POT PIE

Total servings: 8 to 10
Preparation time: 45 minutes
Challenge level: Easy

2 (8-ounce) containers
refrigerated crescent
rolls

1 (15-ounce) jar Alfredo
sauce

2 (12.5-ounce) cans
chunk chicken breast,
drained

1 (15-ounce) can mixed
vegetables

8 ounces shredded
mozzarella cheese

Salt and black pepper to
taste

Required equipment:
10-inch camp Dutch
oven

Preparation at camp:

1. Prepare 21 coals for the Dutch oven.
2. Evenly line bottom of Dutch oven with contents from one package of crescent roll dough.
3. Spread Alfredo sauce over dough.
4. Evenly distribute chicken, canned vegetables, and cheese over Alfredo sauce. Add salt and black pepper to taste.
5. Use dough from second crescent roll package to form top crust.
6. Bake for about 30 minutes using 14 coals on the lid and 7 briquettes under the oven, until the top turns a light golden brown.

Brad Hanson
Crane, Missouri

ADIRONDACK MAC AND CHEESE

V-LO

Total servings: 4 to 6
Preparation time: 30 minutes
Challenge level: Easy

Preparation at camp:

1. Add evaporated milk, cheese, cornstarch, ground mustard, and black pepper to standard Dutch oven over medium heat. Stir frequently while the cheese melts.

2. Bring the cheese sauce to a simmer. Continue to cook for about 2 minutes while stirring constantly.

3. Once the cheese melts and the sauce has thickened, add pasta. Gently stir.

4. Let sit for a few minutes, then stir again and crush Ritz crackers over the top of the mac and cheese.

Ken Harbison
Rochester, New York

1 (12-ounce) can evaporated milk

1 pound sharp cheddar, Gruyere, or Monterey Jack cheese, cut into cubes

2 tablespoons cornstarch

1 teaspoon ground mustard

½ teaspoon ground black pepper

2 (8.5-ounce) packages Barilla Ready Pasta elbow noodles

1 sleeve Ritz crackers

Required equipment:
Medium-size standard Dutch oven

ONE-POT SPAGHETTI AND MEATBALLS

Total servings: 8 to 10
Preparation time: 30 minutes
Challenge level: Easy

1 (45-ounce) jar pasta sauce (your favorite)

1 quart water

1 tablespoon olive oil

1 (16-ounce) package angel hair pasta

1 pound frozen meatballs, thawed

Grated Parmesan cheese to taste

Required equipment:
Medium-size standard Dutch oven

Preparation at camp:
1. Pour pasta sauce, water, and oil into a standard Dutch oven and stir. Bring to a low boil over medium-high heat.
2. Break pasta in half and add to the sauce. Stir until all pasta is coated with sauce.
3. Add meatballs, then reduce heat to a simmer. Stir frequently to prevent pasta from sticking to the bottom.
4. Continue stirring until pasta is al dente, adding additional water if needed.
5. Serve with Parmesan cheese.

Christine and Tim Conners
Tucson, Arizona

PORCUPINE TOMATO SOUP

Total servings: 8 to 10
Preparation time: 1 hour
Challenge level: Easy

This is great first-time recipe for kids!

Preparation at camp:

1. Combine beef, onion, rice, salt, and egg in a bowl. Using clean hands, mix the ingredients well.
2. Form beef mixture into bite-size balls.
3. Meanwhile, combine tomato soup and water in a standard Dutch oven and bring to a boil over high heat.
4. Gently drop porcupine balls into the hot soup.
5. Reduce heat, cover, and simmer for about 30 minutes, until meatballs are cooked through.
6. Serve, topping with shredded cheese to taste.

Tip:
Use an empty soup can to measure the water: just fill it three times for a quart.

Kathleen Kirby
Milltown, New Jersey

2 pounds lean ground beef

1 medium-size onion, chopped

2 cups Minute white rice

½ teaspoon salt

1 egg

3 (10.75-ounce) cans condensed tomato soup

1 quart water

Shredded cheddar cheese to taste

Required equipment:
Medium-size standard Dutch oven
Large mixing bowl

GRILLED BANANA AND PEANUT BUTTER SANDWICH

V-LO

Total servings: 1
Preparation time: 20 minutes
Challenge level: Easy

2 tablespoons butter

2 tablespoons peanut butter

2 slices whole wheat bread

1 banana, thinly sliced

Required equipment:
Small skillet

Preparation at camp:

1. Melt butter in skillet over medium heat.
2. Spread peanut butter over one slice of bread.
3. Press banana slices into peanut butter.
4. Cover with the second slice of bread.
5. Fry sandwich for a few minutes on each side until heated through.

Tip:
Scale the recipe as needed for your group size!

Christine and Tim Conners
Tucson, Arizona

CHICKEN AVOCADO WRAPS

Total servings: 2
Preparation time: 30 minutes
Challenge level: Easy

Preparation at camp:

1. Warm oil in skillet over medium heat.
2. Slice chicken breast into strips, and chop bacon into small pieces.
3. Fry chicken and bacon until no pink remains in the chicken meat.
4. Add salt and black pepper to taste, then remove pan from heat.
5. In a bowl, combine mayonnaise and dill weed.
6. Evenly divide chicken mixture, mayonnaise mixture, lettuce, tomatoes, and avocado among the 4 tortillas.
7. Fold tortillas and serve.

Christine and Tim Conners
Tucson, Arizona

1 teaspoon olive oil

1 large chicken breast

4 slices bacon

Salt and black pepper to taste

⅓ cup mayonnaise

1 tablespoon dried dill weed

2 leaves romaine lettuce, chopped

1 large tomato, chopped

1 avocado, chopped

4 tortillas

Required equipment:
Small skillet
Small mixing bowl

CAMP QUESADILLAS

Total servings: 2
Preparation time: 30 minutes
Challenge level: Easy

This is a simple lunch recipe that can be easily scaled to larger groups and to any unique preferences.

1 tablespoon olive oil

½ cup shredded cheese (your choice)

1 (10-ounce) can water-packed chunk chicken, drained and broken into pieces

¼ cup pico de gallo

4 8-inch tortillas

Optional: sour cream, guacamole, avocado slices, chopped lettuce, sliced olives, black beans, canned corn

Required equipment:
Large skillet
Small mixing bowl

Preparation at camp:

1. Warm oil in skillet over medium heat.
2. Combine cheese, chicken, and pico de gallo in a bowl.
3. Divide chicken mixture between two tortillas, spreading evenly over both. Cover each with the remaining two tortillas, pressing down.
4. Set quesadillas in hot oil, cover the pan, and allow tortillas to cook for a few minutes.
5. Carefully flip each quesadilla to warm the other side.
6. After a few minutes, remove from pan and cut each quesadilla into wedges.
7. Serve with optional ingredients.

Christine and Tim Conners
Tucson, Arizona

ASIAN TURKEY WRAPS

Total servings: 3 to 4
Preparation time: 30 minutes
Challenge level: Easy

Preparation at camp:
1. Warm oil in skillet over medium heat.
2. Fry turkey until fully cooked, with no pink remaining.
3. Add bell pepper, water chestnuts, onions, peanuts, and sauce to the pan and stir. Continue frying until bell pepper is soft.
4. Form "bowls" out of the lettuce leaves and scoop turkey mixture into them.
5. Top the lettuce wraps with cilantro and serve.

Christine and Tim Conners
Tucson, Arizona

1 tablespoon olive oil

1 pound ground turkey

1 green bell pepper, chopped

1 (8-ounce) can water chestnuts, drained and diced

3 green onions, chopped

¼ cup dry-roasted peanuts, chopped

1 (8-ounce) package lettuce wrap sauce

1 head Bibb or butter lettuce

1 small bunch fresh cilantro, stemmed and chopped

Required equipment:
Large skillet

MAGGOT BURGERS

Total servings: 4
Preparation time: 30 minutes
Challenge level: Easy

Please remain calm! No maggots were harmed in the creation of this recipe! All kidding aside, the big event here is that the juice from the meat swells the noodles, causing them to hang out of the burgers like maggots. Yep, eeew indeed. Silly and fun, this recipe is also practical because it tastes great!

1 pound ground beef

½ cup dried chow mein noodles

Salt and black pepper to taste

1 tablespoon olive oil

4 hamburger buns

Toppings: cheese slices, sliced tomatoes, sliced onions, lettuce, ketchup, mayonnaise, yellow mustard

Required equipment:
Large skillet
Medium-size mixing bowl

Preparation at camp:

1. In a bowl, combine ground beef with chow mein noodles. Add salt and ground black pepper to taste.
2. Form ground beef mixture into 4 patties.
3. Warm oil in skillet over medium heat.
4. Fry burgers in oil until no pink remains.
5. Serve on buns with toppings of your choice.

Donna Pettigrew
Anderson, Indiana

VAGABOND TACOS

Total servings: 4
Preparation time: 30 minutes
Challenge level: Easy

Preparation at camp:
1. Cook ground beef in skillet over medium heat.
2. Stir taco seasoning and water into the ground beef. Remove from heat and allow to cool for a few minutes.
3. With the chip bags still sealed, carefully crush corn chips in the bag.
4. Cut each bag open along one side.
5. Add beef mix, lettuce, tomato, cheese, salsa, and sour cream to the chip bags, evenly dividing between each bag.
6. Eat straight from the bag with a fork!

Millie Hutchison
Pittsburgh, Pennsylvania

1 pound lean ground beef or turkey

1 (1-ounce) package taco seasoning mix

¾ cup water

4 (2-ounce) single-serving bags corn chips

1 cup shredded lettuce

1 tomato, chopped

1 cup shredded cheddar cheese

¼ cup salsa

¼ cup sour cream

Required equipment:
Medium-size skillet

NORTH SHORE BARBECUE QUESADILLA

Total servings: 4
Preparation time: 30 minutes
Challenge level: Easy

2 small jalapeño
peppers, chopped

½ bunch fresh cilantro,
stemmed and chopped

1 (10-ounce) can chunk
chicken breast, drained

1 (8-ounce) can crushed
unsweetened pineapple,
drained

¼ cup barbecue sauce

2 cups shredded
Monterey Jack cheese

8 large flour tortillas

¼ cup vegetable oil

Required equipment:
Medium-size skillet
Medium-size mixing
bowl

Preparation at camp:

1. In a bowl, combine jalapeños, cilantro,
   chicken breast, pineapple, barbecue sauce,
   and cheese. Mix well, breaking up any
   chunks.

2. Divide chicken mixture among 4 tortillas,
   covering them evenly. Cover each with the
   remaining tortillas, pressing down.

3. In a skillet over medium heat, fry one
   quesadilla using about 1 tablespoon of
   oil. Cook each side until a golden brown.
   Repeat for each quesadilla.

4. Slice each quesadilla into wedges.

Christine and Tim Conners
Tucson, Arizona

COZUMEL FISH TACOS

Total servings: 4
Preparation time: 30 minutes
Challenge level: Moderate

Preparation at camp:
1. Warm oil in skillet over medium heat.
2. Fry fish, breaking it into smaller pieces as it cooks. Once fish is cooked through, set aside.
3. Cut the lime in half and squeeze one of the halves into a bowl. Slice the remaining half into smaller pieces.
4. Add crema Mexicana to bowl with lime juice. Stir well and set aside.
5. Place crumbled queso fresco, pico de gallo, chopped cabbage, jalapeños, cilantro, and lime pieces on separate plates or in small bowls.
6. Using tortillas, build tacos to taste.

Christine and Tim Conners
Tucson, Arizona

2 tablespoons olive oil

12 ounces whitefish (cod, haddock, halibut, or mahi-mahi)

1 lime

1 cup crema Mexicana

½ cup crumbled queso fresco

1 cup pico de gallo

2 cups chopped cabbage

2 small jalapeño peppers, chopped

1 small bunch fresh cilantro, stemmed and chopped

8 small corn or flour tortillas

Required equipment:
Medium-size skillet
Small mixing bowl

CAST IRON FAJITAS

Total servings: 4 to 6
Preparation time: 30 minutes
Challenge level: Moderate

2 tablespoons vegetable oil

1 pound boneless chicken

1 medium-size onion

1 medium-size red bell pepper

2 teaspoons chili powder

1½ teaspoons ground cumin

½ teaspoon garlic powder

½ teaspoon dried oregano

¼ teaspoon seasoned salt

1 (10-ounce) can diced tomatoes with green chilies

12 corn or small flour tortillas

Optional toppings: chopped lettuce, pico de gallo, sour cream, shredded cheese, guacamole

Required equipment:
Large skillet

Preparation at camp:
1. Warm oil in skillet over medium heat.
2. Slice chicken, onion, and bell pepper into thin strips.
3. Add chicken, chili powder, cumin, garlic powder, oregano, and seasoned salt to pan. Toss chicken and stir to cover in spice blend.
4. Fry chicken until it is fully cooked with no pink remaining.
5. Add tomatoes along with onion and bell pepper strips to pan. Stir well and continue to cook until onions are soft.
6. Serve with tortillas and optional toppings.

Options:
This recipe can be used to make tacos, burritos, or tostadas.

Robert "Cowboy Bob" Dowdy
Great Falls, Montana

BUCKAROO'S ENCHILADA

Total servings: 6
Preparation time: 20 minutes
Challenge level: Easy

Preparation at camp:

1. Warm oil in skillet over medium heat.
2. Slice or tear tortillas into bite-size pieces.
3. Fry tortilla pieces along with the chunk chicken.
4. When tortillas begin to brown, add black beans, diced tomatoes, tomato sauce, and enchilada sauce. Stir well.
5. Once ingredients are heated through, evenly sprinkle shredded cheese into the pan. Do not stir.
6. Cover pan with lid or foil and continue cooking until cheese is melted.
7. Serve with optional toppings.

Robert "Cowboy Bob" Dowdy
Great Falls, Montana

2 tablespoons olive oil

12 corn tortillas

2 (12-ounce) cans chunk chicken breast, drained

1 (15-ounce) can black beans, rinsed and drained

1 (10-ounce) can diced tomatoes with green chilies

1 (8-ounce) can tomato sauce

1 (10-ounce) can red enchilada sauce

1½ cups shredded queso quesadilla cheese

Optional toppings: sliced avocado, fresh cilantro, chopped jalaleño peppers, chopped green onions, sour cream

Required equipment:
Large skillet

KICKED UP SLOPPY JOES

Total servings: 6
Preparation time: 30 minutes
Challenge level: Easy

1 pound ground turkey

4 slices bacon, chopped

1 red bell pepper, chopped

1 green bell pepper, chopped

1 small yellow onion, diced

1 tablespoon barbecue sauce

1 (24-ounce) can Manwich sloppy joe sauce

1 (8.5-ounce) can corn, drained

Hot sauce to taste

1 large bag potato chips

Required equipment:
Large skillet

Preparation at camp:

1. In a large skillet, fry turkey with bacon over medium heat.
2. Once turkey is no longer pink, add peppers and onion and cook until vegetables are soft.
3. Stir barbecue sauce and sloppy joe sauce into the meat and vegetables.
4. Continue to cook until the sauce begins to thicken. Stir in corn, then remove from heat.
5. Distribute potato chips in bowls and ladle the sloppy joe mix over the chips. Add hot sauce to taste.

Options:
Tortilla or corn chips can be substituted for the potato chips.

Ken Spiegel
Medford, New York

MOUNTAIN MAN MAC AND CHEESE

Total servings: 6 to 8
Preparation time: 45 minutes
Challenge level: Easy

Preparation at camp:

1. Warm oil in skillet over medium heat.
2. Chop chicken breast into small pieces.
3. Add chicken and seasoning to the pan and toss until chicken is coated in spice and oil.
4. Cook chicken thoroughly, until no pink remains. Remove chicken from pan and set aside.
5. Combine milk, flour, and butter in the pan. Cook until the mixture thickens, stirring often.
6. Add cheese to the pan. Stir well.
7. Return cooked chicken to the pan. Add pasta and pico de gallo.
8. Continue to cook, stirring often, until ingredients are heated through and pasta has softened.

Option:
Cajun seasoning can be substituted for the Southwest seasoning.

Tip:
Be sure to use precooked pasta for this recipe!

Mike "Mountain Man Mike" Lancaster
Clovis, California

1 tablespoon olive oil

1 chicken breast

1 tablespoon Southwest-style seasoning

2 cups whole milk

3 tablespoons all-purpose flour

3 tablespoons butter

1 (8-ounce) package shredded pepper jack cheese

2 (8.5-ounce) packages Barilla Ready Pasta elbow noodles

2¼ cups pico de gallo

Required equipment:
Large skillet

PIE IRON CALZONE

Total servings: 1
Preparation time: 20 minutes
Challenge level: Moderate

1 teaspoon olive oil

1 premade refrigerated pie dough

2 tablespoons pizza sauce

4 slices pepperoni

1 slice mozzarella cheese

Required equipment:
Pie iron

Preparation at camp:

1. Coat inside of the pie iron with olive oil.
2. Cut out two rectangular pieces of pie dough large enough to fit inside pie iron.
3. Position one of the pieces of pie dough in one side of the pie iron.
4. Top the dough in pie iron with sauce, pepperoni, and cheese. Fold cheese slice if necessary so that it fits.
5. Lay second dough piece over the ingredients in the pie iron and seal the edges of the two pieces of dough together.
6. Close the iron and cook for about 5 minutes on each side over the heat of a campfire or grill. Do not hold the pie iron directly in the flame for an extended length of time or the dough may burn.
7. Remove iron from heat, open the iron, and very carefully remove the contents.

Tip:
This recipe is appropriate for a pie iron roughly 4 by 4 inches square. For a pie iron of different size, scale the ingredients accordingly, remembering that precision isn't critical here.

Christine and Tim Conners
Tucson, Arizona

CHICKEN POT PIE IRON

Total servings: 1
Preparation time: 20 minutes
Challenge level: Moderate

Preparation at camp:
1. Coat inside of the pie iron with butter.
2. Cut out two rectangular pieces of pie dough large enough to fit inside pie iron.
3. Position one of the pieces of pie dough in one side of the pie iron.
4. Top the dough in pie iron with chicken à la king, centering it toward the middle of the dough and away from the edges.
5. Lay second dough piece over the ingredients in the pie iron and tightly seal the edges of the two pieces of dough together.
6. Close the iron and cook for about 5 minutes on each side over the heat of a campfire or grill. Do not hold the pie iron directly in the flame for an extended length of time or the dough may burn.
7. Remove iron from heat, open the iron, and very carefully remove the contents.

Tip:
This recipe is appropriate for a pie iron roughly 4 by 4 inches square. For a pie iron of different size, scale the ingredients accordingly, remembering that precision isn't critical here.

Christine and Tim Conners
Tucson, Arizona

1 teaspoon butter

1 premade refrigerated pie dough

3 tablespoons Swanson Chicken à la King

Required equipment:
Pie iron

Dinner

3-IN-1 CORNISH GAME HEN

Total servings: 2
Preparation time: 1 hour 45 minutes
Challenge level: Difficult

This dinner recipe comes with a bonus: a side dish and a dessert!

1 Cornish game hen, thawed

Salt to taste

Lemon pepper to taste

Ground cayenne pepper to taste

2 slices bacon, cut in half

1 potato, sliced

1 onion, chopped

2 medium-size carrots, peeled and cut into sticks

1 green bell pepper, chopped

3 tablespoons butter, softened

Ground black pepper to taste

1 apple, cored and sliced into thin wedges

2 tablespoons brown sugar

2 tablespoons all-purpose flour

1 cup whole milk

Preparation at camp:

1. Preheat Dutch oven over 21 coals.
2. Prepare hen by rinsing then patting dry with paper towels.
3. Season hen with salt, lemon pepper, and cayenne pepper to taste.
4. Tie legs of the hen together with butcher twine.
5. Drape one piece of bacon on top of each leg and place two pieces across the breast to cover it.
6. Set potato, onion, carrots, and bell pepper on a long sheet of heavy-duty aluminum foil, about 24 inches in length.
7. Add 2 tablespoons butter to the vegetables, spreading the butter about, then sprinkle with salt and black pepper to taste.
8. Fold foil over vegetables, sealing the edges tightly. The "drugstore wrap" technique is a good one to use here. The packet needs to sit vertically in the oven, so make sure the width of the packet is not larger than the height of the walls of the oven.
9. Place sliced apples on a second sheet of long foil with the remaining 1 tablespoon of butter and the brown sugar. Seal tightly, as with the first packet.
10. Carefully set foil packets in the preheated oven, fitting them against the inside wall.
11. Place the hen on a small rack or trivet in the center of the oven, breast-side up, with bacon pieces in place. Ensure there is space between the hen and the foil packets so that air can circulate for even cooking.
12. Move 14 coals to the lid and keep 7 coals under the oven.

13. Bake for 1 hour, rotating the oven and the lid a quarter turn every 15 minutes or so without removing the lid. Hen is ready once the internal temperature reaches at least 165°F. Refresh coals as needed.

14. Remove hen and foil packets and set aside. Pour off the drippings from the oven, reserving about 2 tablespoons in the oven. Place oven back over the coals.

15. Add flour and a pinch of black pepper to the oven, stirring until smooth. Gradually add milk to the oven, continuously stirring until thickened. Crumble cooked bacon pieces into the oven.

16. Split the hen between two plates. Divide the vegetable pack and pour the gravy over the vegetables. Save the stewed apples until dessert!

Tip:
The bacon in this recipe protects the breast and legs from burning while self-basting the hen during cooking.

Keith Williams
Sharpsburg, Georgia

Required equipment:
10-inch camp Dutch oven
Trivet or small rack
Heavy-duty aluminum foil
Butcher's twine

AROUND-THE-WORLD PIZZA

Total servings: 2
Preparation time: 45 minutes
Challenge level: Easy

You can make pizza at camp just as easily as you can make it at home! The toppings are endless, so we've offered a few suggestions to take you around the world!

1 (13.8-ounce) container Pillsbury refrigerated pizza crust

Italian Margherita Pizza:
Pizza sauce

Mozzarella cheese balls, sliced

Fresh basil

Tomato slices

Greek Pizza:
Olive oil

Feta cheese

Tomato slices

Artichoke hearts

Kalamata olive slices

Fresh spinach

Hawaiian Pizza:
Pizza sauce

Cooked ham or Canadian bacon

Pineapple chunks

New York Buffalo Chicken Pizza:
Buffalo wing sauce

Precooked or canned chicken

Mozzarella cheese balls, sliced

Blue cheese dressing

Red onion slices

Hot sauce

Required equipment:
10-inch camp Dutch oven

Preparation at camp:
1. Prepare 25 coals for the Dutch oven.
2. Unroll the dough and press it evenly into the bottom of a greased Dutch oven, creating a raised edge around the perimeter.
3. Start by baking only the crust using 17 coals on the lid and 8 coals under the oven bottom for about 8 minutes.
4. Remove the lid and move the oven from the coals.
5. Carefully add your favorite toppings to the pizza crust.
6. Replace the lid, with the coals still on it, and bake for another 10 minutes or until the crust is a golden brown.

Christine and Tim Conners
Tucson, Arizona

GET-A-SPOUSE SOUR CREAM CHICKEN

Total servings: 3 to 4
Preparation time: 1 hour 30 minutes
Challenge level: Moderate

This was the first recipe I prepared for my wife when we began dating back in 1982. It remains a go-to at our home!

Preparation at camp:

1. Prepare 21 coals for the Dutch oven.
2. Sprinkle chicken with seasoned salt to taste, then coat using 2 tablespoons flour.
3. Melt 4 tablespoons butter in Dutch oven over coals.
4. Brown chicken thighs on both sides, then set aside.
5. Melt 3 more tablespoons butter in the oven, then stir in 2 tablespoons flour to make a roux.
6. Blend in sour cream and chicken stock.
7. Bring to a low simmer and add seasoned salt to taste. Stir well.
8. Return the chicken to the oven and add the potatoes.
9. Cover oven and move 14 coals to the lid, leaving 7 coals under the oven. Refresh coals as necessary.
10. Cook for about 45 minutes. Chicken is ready once internal temperature reaches 165°F.

1 pound chicken thighs

Seasoned salt to taste

4 tablespoons all-purpose flour

7 tablespoons butter

1 cup sour cream

1 cup chicken stock

4 red new potatoes, cut into ¾-inch cubes

Required equipment:
10-inch camp Dutch oven

Robert "Cowboy Bob" Dowdy
Great Falls, Montana

MOONSHADOW MUSSELS

Total servings: 4
Preparation time: 45 minutes
Challenge level: Easy

I first began cooking with mussels while living in New Zealand, where mollusks are prevalent. We were there because we were expecting our second child. We had been sailing our 40-foot wooden sailboat across the Pacific on a trip that would end up taking us around the world and then some. We were anchored aboard the good ship Moonshadow *in Whangarei, north of the Bay of Plenty. We assimilated ourselves into the local culture, and there we discovered green mussels. They were inexpensive, so they fit into our limited budget. What a treat! This recipe came about by experimentation and out of whatever could be gathered and tossed in the pot.*

2 teaspoons olive oil

2 teaspoons minced garlic

¼ cup dry white wine

1 teaspoon fresh lemon or lime juice

¼ teaspoon crushed red pepper

1 (14.5-ounce) can no-salt-added stewed tomatoes, undrained and chopped

2 (6.5-ounce) cans minced clams with juice

2 pounds small mussels, scrubbed and debearded (preferably fresh, or frozen and uncooked)

2 tablespoons chopped fresh flat-leaf parsley

Required equipment:
12-inch camp Dutch oven

Preparation at camp:

1. Heat olive oil in Dutch oven over 17 coals.
2. Add garlic, then sauté for 1 minute.
3. Add wine, citrus juice, red pepper, tomatoes, and clams with the juice. Stir and bring to a boil.
4. Add mussels, then cover, reduce half the coals, and simmer for 5 minutes or until shells open.
5. Remove from heat and discard any mussels with unopened shells.
6. Stir in parsley and serve.

Options:
Enjoy with French bread, or ladle over pasta or rice.

David Fischer
Stuart, Florida

BAHAMA BEACH SPICED RIBS

Total servings: 4
Preparation time: 2 hours
Challenge level: Moderate

Preparation at camp:

1. Prepare 21 coals for the Dutch oven.
2. Cut each rib into pieces roughly 4 inches in length.
3. In a bowl, blend black pepper, cayenne pepper, paprika, ginger, allspice, cinnamon, garlic powder, ground mustard, and minced onion.
4. Thoroughly rub the spice mix onto each piece of meat.
5. Pour water into Dutch oven and layer the spiced ribs and sliced onions within.
6. Cover and cook for 1½ hours using 14 coals on the lid and 7 coals under the oven. Refresh coals as required.
7. With oven still over the coals, remove lid and pour barbecue sauce over ribs.
8. Return coal-covered lid to the oven and continue cooking for an additional 15 minutes.

C. Phillip Jones
Morrisville, North Carolina

2 pounds country-style pork loin ribs

½ teaspoon ground black pepper

½ teaspoon ground cayenne pepper

½ teaspoon paprika

½ teaspoon ground ginger

1 teaspoon allspice

1 teaspoon ground cinnamon

1 teaspoon garlic powder

2 teaspoons ground mustard

2 tablespoons dried minced onion

½ cup water

1 medium-size onion, sliced into thin rings

1 cup barbecue sauce

Required equipment:
10-inch camp Dutch oven
Small mixing bowl

CHICKEN CHUTNEY

Total servings: 4 to 6
Preparation time: 1 hour 15 minutes
Challenge level: Easy

1 whole chicken

1 (9-ounce) jar Major Grey's chutney

Required equipment:
12-inch camp Dutch oven

Preparation at camp:
1. Prepare 31 coals for the Dutch oven.
2. Set chicken in Dutch oven and pour chutney over top of chicken. Set lid on the oven.
3. Using 21 coals on the lid and 10 coals under the oven, bake for about 1 hour, until chicken is fully cooked with an internal temperature of at least 165°F. Refresh coals as required.

Tip:
The deeper interior of larger Dutch ovens, such as the 12-inch specified here, is usually required to cook whole birds or larger cuts of meat. However, chopping the chicken into smaller pieces prior to cooking, or using a smaller bird, will permit the use of a smaller Dutch oven. Whatever your method, do not force a cut of meat to fit within an oven! If you do, any portion of meat in contact with the underside of the lid will burn.

Christine and Tim Conners
Tucson, Arizona

ITALIAN STUFFED PEPPERS

Total servings: 6
Preparation time: 1 hour
Challenge level: Easy

V-LO

Preparation at camp:

1. Prepare 21 coals for the Dutch oven.
2. Cut tops from bell peppers, then remove the seeds and webs.
3. Set peppers upright in Dutch oven. If your peppers are too tall, trim a bit from the height so they'll fit with the lid on.
4. In a bowl, combine oil, rice, cheese roll pieces, Italian seasoning, crushed tomatoes, and cilantro. Mix well.
5. With a spoon, evenly scoop rice mixture into each pepper.
6. Bake using 14 coals on the lid and 7 coals under the oven for about 30 minutes or until the peppers are soft and the rice is heated through.

Tip:
Mozzarella rolls can be found in the gourmet cheese section at the grocery store.

Christine and Tim Conners
Tucson, Arizona

6 small red or green bell peppers

1 tablespoon olive oil

1 (8.8-ounce) package Ben's Original long grain white Ready Rice

2 (8-ounce) packages mozzarella-prosciutto-basil rolls, cut into small pieces

1 tablespoon Italian seasoning blend

1 (15-ounce) can crushed tomatoes

1 bunch fresh cilantro, stemmed and chopped

Required equipment:
10-inch camp Dutch oven
Medium-size mixing bowl

MOUNTAIN LAKE STUFFED GAME HENS

Total servings: 4 to 8
Preparation time: 2 hours
Challenge level: Moderate

I can guarantee this will be one of the most hearty, savory, and flavorful Dutch oven meals you have ever eaten. Tastes even more amazing when enjoyed on the shore of a mountain lake!

4 Cornish game hens, thawed

3 tablespoons butter

4 tablespoons olive oil

Seasoned salt to taste

Ground black pepper to taste

3 cloves garlic, minced

4 small sweet onions, quartered

2 (8.8-ounce) packages Ben's Original long grain and wild Ready Rice

2 cups dry white wine

Preparation at camp:

1. Prepare 25 coals for the Dutch oven.
2. Wash the hens and pat dry with paper towels.
3. Rub inside of birds using about 1 tablespoon of the butter.
4. Use about 1 tablespoon of the oil to fully coat the skin of the hens.
5. Generously sprinkle seasoned salt and black pepper over the outside of the hens.
6. In Dutch oven over 25 coals, add remainder of the butter along with remainder of the oil. Stir as butter melts.
7. Fry the garlic and onions in oven. Once onion caramelizes and garlic turns light brown, add hens to the oven and fry the skin of the birds to a light golden brown, turning frequently to cook all sides.
8. Remove oven from heat and carefully place hens leg-side up in oven.
9. Spoon caramelized onions and garlic evenly into each bird cavity.
10. Add 3 to 4 tablespoons Ready Rice to inside of each hen. Pour remainder of rice around the birds.
11. Pour wine over rice.

12. Move 17 coals to the lid, keeping 8 coals under the oven.
13. Bake for 1½ hours or until the birds reach an internal temperature of 165°F. Be sure to refresh coals as needed to keep the baking process going.

Option:
Chicken broth can be substituted for the white wine.

Chad Jones
Athol, Idaho

Required equipment:
12-inch camp Dutch oven

ASIAN-STYLE SPARE RIBS

Total servings: 6
Preparation time: 1 hour 15 minutes
Challenge level: Easy

3 pounds St. Louis–style pork spare ribs

1 cup soy sauce

½ cup brown sugar

1 tablespoon Chinese 5-spice blend

¼ cup rice vinegar

2 tablespoons fresh minced ginger

4 cloves garlic, minced

1 teaspoon crushed red pepper

Required equipment:
10-inch camp Dutch oven
Medium-size mixing bowl

Preparation at camp:

1. Prepare 21 coals for the Dutch oven.
2. Separate ribs into individual pieces along the bone.
3. Stack ribs in Dutch oven.
4. In a bowl, combine soy sauce, brown sugar, Chinese 5-spice blend, rice vinegar, ginger, garlic, and crushed red pepper. Stir well.
5. Pour soy-spice mixture over ribs in oven.
6. Bake using 14 coals on the lid and 7 coals under the oven for about 1 hour or until the internal temperature of the meat reaches 145°F. Refresh coals as needed.

Christine and Tim Conners
Tucson, Arizona

LAZY LASAGNA

Total servings: 6 to 8
Preparation time: 30 minutes
Challenge level: Easy

V-LO

Preparation at camp:
1. In Dutch oven over 21 coals, combine pasta, ricotta, Parmesan cheese, pasta sauce, Italian seasoning, and 1 cup of mozzarella cheese. Mix well.
2. Evenly spread the second cup of mozzarella cheese over the top.
3. Move 14 of the coals to the lid of the oven, keeping 7 coals under the oven.
4. Bake for about 10 to 15 minutes or until the cheese is melted and slightly brown.

Options:
Any optional vegetables can be cooked first then added to step 1. Try sliced mushrooms, chopped onions, chopped bell pepper, minced garlic, or fresh basil!

Ken Spiegel
Medford, New York

3 (8.5-ounce) packages Barilla Ready Pasta rotini noodles

1 (15-ounce) container ricotta cheese

½ cup grated Parmesan cheese

1 (24-ounce) jar pasta sauce (your favorite)

2 tablespoons Italian seasoning blend

2 cups shredded mozzarella cheese

Required equipment:
10-inch camp Dutch oven

DELUGE SALMON BAKE

Total servings: 6 to 8
Preparation time: 45 minutes
Challenge level: Easy

I successfully cooked this recipe outside in a torrential downpour. Five minutes into the bake, the heavens opened. I frantically dragged a tarp over the whole thing, and for 30 minutes I diverted rain from the coals!

2 pounds salmon fillets

2 tablespoons olive oil

1 pinch dried basil

3 cloves garlic, minced

1 small onion, sliced into thin rings

1 (14.5-ounce) can diced tomatoes with green chilies

1 (15-ounce) can lima beans or green beans, drained

Required equipment:
10-inch camp Dutch oven

Preparation at camp:

1. Prepare 21 coals for the Dutch oven.
2. Evenly arrange salmon fillets in a well-oiled Dutch oven, skin-side down.
3. Drizzle olive oil over the fillets.
4. Cover salmon with all the remaining ingredients, ending with the beans on top.
5. Using 14 coals on the lid and 7 coals under the oven, bake for about 30 minutes, until edge of fish flakes easily with a fork and internal temperature is at least 145°F.

Max Coles
Richmond Hill, Virginia

STARRY NIGHT VEGETARIAN CHILI

Total servings: 6 to 8
Preparation time: 45 minutes
Challenge level: Easy

V

Preparation at camp:
1. Warm oil in Dutch oven over 13 coals.
2. Add onion, bell pepper, and garlic. Sauté until tender.
3. Add remaining ingredients. Stir well.
4. Continue cooking for about 20 minutes, stirring occasionally.
5. Serve with optional toppings.

Christine and Tim Conners
Tucson, Arizona

1 teaspoon olive oil

1 onion, chopped

1 green bell pepper, chopped

3 cloves garlic, minced

2 jalapeño peppers, diced

1 tablespoon dried oregano

2 teaspoons chili powder

1 teaspoon ground cumin

1 teaspoon ground coriander

1 (28-ounce) can diced tomatoes, drained

1 (15-ounce) can tomato sauce

2 teaspoons granulated sugar

2 (15-ounce) cans three-bean blend

Optional toppings: sour cream, chopped green onions, shredded cheese

Required equipment:
12-inch camp Dutch oven

MEXICAN PIE

Total servings: 6 to 8
Preparation time: 1 hour 15 minutes
Challenge level: Easy

1 tablespoon olive oil

1 pound ground turkey

1 onion, diced

12 corn tortillas

1 (15-ounce) can black beans, rinsed and drained

1 (16-ounce) jar salsa

8 ounces Mexican blend shredded cheese

8 ounces sour cream

Required equipment:
10-inch camp Dutch oven

Preparation at camp:

1. Warm oil in Dutch oven over 21 coals.

2. Cook ground turkey and onion until no pink remains in the meat. Remove turkey and onions from oven and set aside.

3. Layer 4 tortillas on the bottom of the oven.

4. Evenly spread ½ of the cooked turkey and onions, ½ of the beans, ⅓ of the salsa, and ⅓ of the cheese over the tortillas.

5. Repeat using a second layer of 4 tortillas, the remainder of the turkey and onions, the remainder of the beans, and ½ of the remaining salsa and cheese.

6. Cover with the remaining 4 tortillas and top with the remaining salsa and cheese.

7. Moving 14 coals to the lid and leaving 7 coals under the oven, bake for about 30 minutes.

8. Once heated through, slices into wedges and serve with dollops of sour cream.

Christine and Tim Conners
Tucson, Arizona

GUADALAJARA DEEP DISH

Total servings: 6 to 8
Preparation time: 1 hour 30 minutes
Challenge level: Easy

I don't consider myself much of a cook. But when I do cook, I use a Dutch oven. It is such a forgiving device. When my kids were small, they loved to join in, especially when I was using a Dutch oven. That's one reason this recipe has become a family favorite!

Preparation at camp:

1. In a Dutch oven over 21 coals, brown the ground beef.
2. Remove oven from the coals and transfer meat to a bowl.
3. Add taco seasoning to the bowl along with the hominy, picante sauce, green chilies, onion, chives, and black olives. Stir well.
4. Set one tortilla in bottom of oven and cover with ½ of the meat mixture, ½ of the sour cream, and ⅓ of the cheese.
5. Repeat this layering process with a second tortilla, topping with the remaining meat mixture and sour cream and half of the remaining cheese.
6. Top with the third tortilla, the remaining cheese, and jalapeños slices.
7. Bake using 14 coals on the lid and 7 coals under the oven for about 30 minutes, until the cheese and contents are simmering.
8. Remove from heat. Allow to rest for 10 minutes before serving.

Victor Rocha
Germantown, Tennessee

1 pound lean ground beef

1 (1-ounce) package taco seasoning mix

1 (15.5-ounce) can white hominy, drained

½ cup picante sauce

1 (4-ounce) can green chilies

1 small onion, chopped

1 handful chopped fresh chives

1 (2.25-ounce) can sliced black olives, drained

3 10-inch flour tortillas

8 ounces sour cream

8 ounces shredded sharp cheddar cheese

2 jalapeño peppers, seeded and sliced into rings

Required equipment:
10-inch camp Dutch oven
Large mixing bowl

BARBECUE MEATLOAF

Total servings: 6 to 8
Preparation time: 1 hour 30 minutes
Challenge level: Moderate

1 pound lean ground
beef

1 small sweet onion,
diced

1 cup dry plain bread
crumbs

2 eggs

1 (18-ounce) bottle
barbecue sauce

1 (16-ounce) package
frozen classic mixed
vegtables, thawed

Salt and black pepper to
taste

Required equipment:
10-inch camp Dutch
oven
Medium-size mixing
bowl

Preparation at camp:

1. Prepare 21 coals for the Dutch oven.

2. Combine ground beef, onion, bread crumbs, eggs, and ¼ cup barbecue sauce in a bowl. Use clean hands to mush the ingredients together until everything is evenly blended.

3. Form the meat mixture into a shape that resembles a small loaf of bread.

4. Set the meatloaf in the middle of Dutch oven, being sure there is a gap between the meat and the walls and lid.

5. Pour the thawed vegetables around the sides of the meatloaf.

6. Bake using 14 coals on the lid and 7 coals under the oven for about 1 hour or until the meat is no longer pink and registers at least 160°F internally. Refresh coals as needed.

7. Once off the coals, pour ¼ cup barbecue sauce over the meatloaf. Add salt and black pepper to taste.

8. Slice the loaf and serve with the vegetables and remaining barbecue sauce.

Christine and Tim Conners
Tucson, Arizona

STEAMBOAT STEW

Total servings: 8
Preparation time: 1 hour
Challenge level: Easy

Steamboat Stew comes from Alma Bludworth, who lived in Freeport, Florida, circa 1905. This is a family recipe that was served on the paddle wheeler Captain Fritz, *which ran freight and passenger service between Freeport and Pensacola in the early 1900s. The* Fritz *was operated for a time by Alma's father and uncle.*

Preparation at camp:

1. In a Dutch oven over 20 coals, brown bacon until cooked but not crispy.
2. Remove bacon and chop into ½-inch pieces.
3. Fry potatoes in the bacon grease until soft.
4. Add onions to the potatoes and cook until onions become translucent.
5. Return bacon to the oven and add milk, butter, salt, and black pepper. Stir gently to avoid mashing the potatoes.
6. Remove a few of the coals and continue cooking for another 5 to 10 minutes. The final consistency should be like a thick stew.

Steve Burleson
Irondale, Alabama

1 pound bacon

8 Idaho potatoes, peeled and sliced into ½-inch cubes

1 large white onion, chopped

1 cup whole milk

½ cup (1 standard stick) salted butter

½ teaspoon salt

2 teaspoons ground black pepper

Required equipment:
12-inch camp Dutch oven

CHICKEN PENNE PASTA

Total servings: 8
Preparation time: 1 hour 15 minutes
Challenge level: Easy

2 tablespoons olive oil

4 boneless, skinless chicken breasts, cut in half

1 teaspoon Italian seasoning blend

2 (8.5-ounce) packages Barilla Ready Pasta penne noodles

1 (24-ounce) jar pasta sauce (your favorite)

4 slices provolone cheese

6 ounces (about 1½ cups) grated Parmesan cheese

Required equipment:
10-inch camp Dutch oven

Preparation at camp:

1. Warm oil in Dutch oven over 21 coals.
2. Add chicken breasts to oven, sprinkle with Italian seasoning, then sear the chicken to a light brown on each side.
3. Remove oven from coals and set chicken aside, leaving the oil and juices in pot.
4. Add pasta and half of the sauce to oven and stir well, covering the pasta.
5. Return chicken to the oven, distributing the pieces over top of pasta.
6. Cover chicken with the remaining sauce.
7. Place ½ slice of provolone cheese on each piece of chicken, then sprinkle Parmesan cheese over all.
8. Bake using 14 coals on the lid and 7 coals under the oven for 30 to 40 minutes, until the internal temperature of the chicken reaches 165°F.

Jeff Gleiser
Madison, North Carolina

MOUNTAIN STEW

Total servings: 8
Preparation time: 1 hour 30 minutes
Challenge level: Easy

A great recipe that permits a lot of variability based on the size and preferences of your group.

Preparation at camp:

1. Preheat Dutch oven over 21 coals.
2. Cook bacon until crispy.
3. Add chicken to the oven and sprinkle with lemon pepper. Stir occasionally until chicken is fully cooked.
4. Add potatoes, onion, and baby carrots to the oven.
5. Turn the meat and vegetables several times, scraping the bacon drippings from the bottom of the oven and coating the vegetables.
6. Move 14 coals to the lid and leave 7 coals under the oven.
7. Bake for about 1 hour, stirring several times initially. After that, leave the stew alone, as additional turning will cause the carrots and potatoes to break apart. Refresh coals as needed. Stew is ready once carrots and potatoes become soft.
8. Add salt to taste, then serve.

1 pound bacon, with slices cut into thirds

4 boneless, skinless chicken breasts, cubed

Lemon pepper to taste

1 pound potatoes, cut into wedges

1 onion, chopped

1 pound baby carrots

Salt to taste

Required equipment:
10-inch camp Dutch oven

Tim Good
Mount Sidney, Virginia

EASTERN SHORES LASAGNA

Total servings: 8
Preparation time: 1 hour 45 minutes
Challenge level: Difficult

This was originally a microwave lasagna recipe that my mother discovered many years ago. I liked it so much, I made it for my wife on our first date, and decades later I adapted it for my Scout troop!

1 (15-ounce) container ricotta cheese

1 egg, beaten

2 tablespoons dried parsley flakes

1 teaspoon salt

⅛ teaspoon ground black pepper

1 tablespoon olive oil

1½ pounds lean ground beef

1 clove garlic, pressed

½ teaspoon dried oregano

½ teaspoon dried sweet basil

½ teaspoon granulated sugar

1 (6-ounce) can tomato paste

1 (5-ounce) can tomato sauce

1¼ cups water

1 small onion, diced

6 sheets Barilla Oven-Ready lasagna noodles

1 pound shredded mozzarella cheese

⅓ cup grated Parmesan cheese

Preparation at camp:

1. Combine ricotta, egg, 1 tablespoon parsley, ½ teaspoon salt, and black pepper in a small bowl. Mix well.

2. Heat oil in Dutch oven over 25 coals.

3. In the hot oven, brown the beef until no pink remains, stirring occasionally.

4. Stir in garlic, remaining 1 tablespoon parsley, remaining ½ teaspoon salt, oregano, basil, sugar, tomato paste, tomato sauce, water, and onion. Heat about 5 minutes, stirring occasionally.

5. Remove oven from coals and very carefully pour sauce into a large bowl. Leave enough sauce to just cover bottom of oven.

6. Add a layer of noodles over sauce in the oven, breaking some of the noodles to fill in the gaps.

7. Pour about ½ of the ricotta mix over the noodles followed by about ⅓ of the mozzarella cheese, about ⅓ of the Parmesan cheese, and ½ of the remaining sauce.

8. Repeat steps 6 and 7. You'll have about ⅓ of the mozzarella and Parmesan cheeses remaining.

9. Using a fresh batch of 25 coals, place 17 coals on the lid and 8 coals under the oven.

10. Bake the lasagne for 45 minutes.

11. Remove the lid, then add the remaining cheeses. Do not stir!

12. Cook for 15 more minutes or until cheese is melted.

Option:

Wrap buttered slices of garlic bread in foil and bake on top of the coals on the lid of the Dutch oven for the final 15 minutes of cooking, flipping the bread halfway through.

David Nelsen
Mechanicsville, Maryland

Required equipment:
12-inch camp Dutch oven
Large mixing bowl
Small mixing bowl

MAMABEE'S PORK ROAST WITH PEACH GLAZE

Total servings: 8
Preparation time: 1 hour 45 minutes (plus 6 hours for marinating)
Challenge level: Difficult

3 pounds pork tenderloin roast

2 cloves garlic, peeled and cut into quarters

½ cup white vinegar

1 teaspoon salt

½ teaspoon ground black pepper

1 teaspoon rubbed sage

½ teaspoon ground marjoram

2 tablespoons olive oil

2 cups chicken broth

1 (18-ounce) jar peach preserves

¼ cup peach nectar

Required equipment:
12-inch camp Dutch oven
Small roasting rack (to fit in oven)
Small mixing bowl
2-gallon ziplock bag

Preparation at camp:

1. Cut about 8 slits in various locations around the top of the roast. Insert garlic pieces into the slits.
2. Place roast in a large ziplock bag along with the vinegar, salt, black pepper, sage, and marjoram. Seal tightly.
3. Marinate roast in a refrigerator or cooler for at least 6 hours. Occasionally rotate and shake the bag to coat the pork.
4. Warm oil in a Dutch oven over 25 coals.
5. Remove roast from bag, then place roast in the hot oil, briefly browning the meat on all sides.
6. Set a small rack under the roast in the oven.
7. Pour chicken broth over the roast.
8. Combine 1 cup of the preserves and the peach nectar in a bowl. Mix well, then evenly pour over the roast.
9. Transfer 17 coals to the lid, leaving 8 coals under the oven. Cooking time will be about 20 to 25 minutes per pound of meat. Refresh coals as needed.
10. After the first 30 minutes, baste roast with marinade from the oven. Continue basting every 15 minutes while the roast is cooking. When done, the roast will have an internal temperature of 145°F.
11. Mix a small amount of pan drippings with the remaining peach preserves to make a glaze to serve with the roast.

Shannon Hutton
Tomball, Texas

EASY ENCHILADAS

Total servings: 8 to 10
Preparation time: 1 hour
Challenge level: Easy

Simple to make but bursting with taste!

Preparation at camp:
1. Prepare 32 coals for the Dutch oven.
2. Line oven with aluminum foil, then grease the foil with oil.
3. Lay ⅓ of the tortilla chips over the bottom of the oven.
4. Pour about ⅓ of the pinto beans and olives (i.e., about ⅔ of a single can) and ⅓ of the enchilada sauce, sour cream, ranch dip mix, shredded chicken, and cheese over the top of the chips.
5. Repeat steps 3 and 4 twice more, using up all the remaining ingredients.
6. Bake for 40 minutes using 21 coals on the lid and 11 underneath the oven or until cheese is melted and bubbly.

William Rose
Wayne, Pennsylvania

1 teaspoon olive oil

1 (12-ounce) bag corn tortilla chips

2 (15-ounce) cans pinto beans, rinsed and drained

2 (2.25-ounce) cans sliced black olives, drained

1 (15-ounce) can green enchilada sauce

1 (16-ounce) container sour cream

1 (1-ounce) package ranch dip mix

1 (22-ounce) package Tyson Grilled & Ready chicken breast strips, shredded

3 cups shredded cheddar cheese

Required equipment:
14-inch camp Dutch oven
Heavy-duty aluminum foil

HIGHLINE PORK LOIN

Total servings: 8 to 10
Preparation time: 2 hours
Challenge level: Difficult

The Uinta Highline is a famous point-to-point trail near our home in Utah. My family and I completed an 82-mile route on the trail, which included a close-up view of Kings Peak, the highest point in Utah.

1 (8.8-ounce) package Ben's Original long grain and wild Ready Rice

2 cups plain cubed stuffing mix

1 cup chopped peeled Granny Smith apple

¼ cup granulated sugar

¼ cup dried cranberries

¼ cup chopped onion

¼ cup (½ standard stick) butter, softened

¼ teaspoon rubbed sage

1 (14.5-ounce) can vegetable broth

Salt and black pepper to taste

4 pounds boneless pork loin roast

Required equipment:
12-inch camp Dutch oven
Medium-size mixing bowl
Butcher's twine

Preparation at camp:

1. Preheat oven with 7 coals under the oven and 16 coals on the lid.

2. In a bowl, combine rice, stuffing mix, apple, sugar, cranberries, onion, butter, sage, and ¼ cup vegetable broth.

3. Mix stuffing blend well, adding salt and black pepper to taste.

4. Referring to the accompanying illustrations, use a sharp knife to create a flat sheet of meat from the boneless pork loin. As the cuts are made, unroll the loin like a sleeping bag.

5. Once pork is carved and laid flat, evenly spread stuffing mixture over the top.

6. Roll meat and stuffing into a cylinder. Tie the roll together using several lengths of butcher's twine.

7. Rub salt and black pepper on outside of pork roll to taste.

8. Set pork roll in center of oven, then pour remainder of broth into oven.

9. Cook roast for 90 minutes. Rotate lid and base a quarter turn in opposite directions every 30 minutes or so to avoid hot spots. Refresh coals as needed.

10. Roast is ready once internal temperature reaches 145°F at its deepest portion. Do not exceed 155°F or roast will begin to dry out.

11. Carefully remove roast from oven and slice into thick disks, each disk a "wheel" of rolled pork with a swirl of apple-rice stuffing.

Tip:
Be sure the oven is well-greased for this recipe.

Brandon Peterson
Pleasant Grove, Illinois

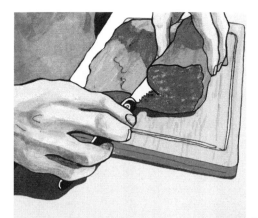

Slicing the loin

Covering the loin with stuffing

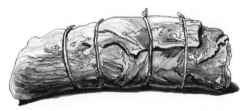

Loin tied with twine

Wheel of the roast ready to serve

STUFFED CAJUN BEEF ROAST

Total servings: 8 to 10
Preparation time: 2 hours
Challenge level: Moderate

2 tablespoons olive oil

4 pounds boneless beef tenderloin

4 slices Swiss cheese

2 (4-ounce) cans sliced mushrooms, drained

½ cup grated Parmesan cheese

¼ cup dried parsley flakes

2 teaspoons seasoned salt

1 tablespoon dried oregano leaves

1 tablespoon ground black pepper

2 teaspoons minced garlic

1 teaspoon crushed red pepper

1 teaspoon chili powder

1 teaspoon ground cumin

8 ounces sour cream

1 cube beef bouillon

1 tablespoon cornstarch

Required equipment:
12-inch camp Dutch oven
Small mixing bowl
Butcher's twine

Preparation at camp:

1. Warm oil in Dutch oven over 25 coals.
2. Slice roast ⅔ of the way through the center lengthwise and lay open.
3. Evenly layer Swiss cheese, mushrooms, Parmesan cheese, and parsley over the meat.
4. Close the roast and tie with several lengths of butcher's twine.
5. Prepare Cajun rub by combining seasoned salt, oregano, black pepper, minced garlic, red pepper, chili powder, and cumin in a bowl. Generously rub over the outside of roast.
6. Place roast in the hot oil and sear the outside on all sides.
7. Move 17 coals to the lid, leaving 8 coals under the oven, and cook for about 90 minutes or until the internal temperature reaches 145°F. Refresh coals as needed.
8. While roast is cooking, prepare the sauce by combining sour cream, bouillon cube, and cornstarch, stirring well and breaking up the bouillon.
9. Serve the roast sliced, topping with sauce to taste.

Paul Wolbeck
Wetumpka, Alabama

CORNED BEEF AND CABBAGE

Total servings: 8 to 10
Preparation time: 2 hours 15 minutes
Challenge level: Difficult

Preparation at camp:
1. Prepare 19 coals for the Dutch oven.
2. Set brisket in center of Dutch oven. Distribute cabbage, carrots, and onion around brisket.
3. In a bowl, combine the black pepper, parsley, garlic powder, allspice, brown sugar, apple juice, and salt. Mix well and pour over the meat and vegetables.
4. Using 13 coals on the lid and 6 coals under the oven, bake for at least 2 hours, refreshing coals as needed. Brisket is fully cooked when it reaches an internal temperature of 145°F.
5. While brisket cooks, prepare the sauce by mixing the horseradish, sour cream, and Dijon mustard in a small bowl.
6. Serve brisket with the sauce.

Tips:
Raw corned beef can be very tough, and so roasting at lower temperatures for longer periods of time is the key to tenderizing. Cooking to a final internal temperature greater than 145°F should improve tenderness, as will allowing it to rest for a while off the coals before slicing.

Christine and Tim Conners
Tucson, Arizona

2½ pounds corned beef brisket

1½ pounds cabbage, cut into large pieces

8 ounces baby carrots

1 onion, cut into wedges

1 teaspoon ground black pepper

1 teaspoon dried parsley flakes

½ teaspoon garlic powder

½ teaspoon allspice

½ cup brown sugar

2 cups apple juice

½ teaspoon salt

2 teaspoons prepared horseradish

½ cup sour cream

2 tablespoons Dijon mustard

Required equipment:
10-inch camp Dutch oven
Medium-size mixing bowl
Small-mixing bowl

CAMPFIRE POTATO PIE

Total servings: 10 to 12
Preparation time: 1 hour 45 minutes
Challenge level: Moderate

1 pound ground beef

1 pound ground pork sausage

1 medium-size onion, chopped

2 teaspoons dried oregano

2 teaspoons dried basil

2 teaspoons Worcestershire sauce

6 medium-size carrots, peeled and sliced

1 (15-ounce) can tomato sauce

3 cups shredded cheddar cheese

4 cloves garlic, minced

3 medium-size potatoes, peeled and sliced

2 (5.5-ounce) cans V8 juice

1½ pounds frozen regular shredded hash browns, thawed

Required equipment:
12-inch camp Dutch oven
Large mixing bowl

Preparation at camp:

1. In a Dutch oven over 25 coals, brown the beef, sausage, and half of the chopped onions.

2. Remove Dutch oven from heat and carefully drain grease.

3. Add oregano, basil, Worcestershire sauce, carrots, tomato sauce, 2 cups of the cheddar cheese, and half of the garlic. Stir well and transfer the meat mixture to a bowl.

4. Lay potato slices evenly in bottom of the oven.

5. Cover potatoes with remaining chopped onions and garlic. Cover all with one can of V8 juice.

6. Return the meat mixture to the oven, spreading evenly over potato layer.

7. Pour second can of V8 juice over the meat mixture.

8. Move 17 coals to the lid and leave 8 coals under the oven. Bake for about 30 minutes, refreshing coals as needed.

9. Uncover oven and spread shredded potatoes over top of the meat mixture.

10. Return lid to the oven and continue to cook for another 30 minutes, until potato slices are soft and shredded potatoes are cooked through.

11. Uncover and spread remaining 1 cup of shredded cheese over the potatoes. Cover for a few minutes until cheese has melted.

Steve Deemer
Indiana, Pennsylvania

CHICKEN SURPRISE

Total servings: 12
Preparation time: 1 hour 45 minutes
Challenge level: Moderate

Preparation at camp:
1. Warm oil in Dutch oven over 25 coals.
2. Sprinkle both sides of the chicken thighs with salt and pepper.
3. Fry chicken in oil for a few minutes, browning the meat on both sides. Cook in batches if necessary.
4. In a bowl, combine the two cans of soup with the water (note that the amount of water needed is equivalent to about 1½ filled soup cans).
5. Once all the pieces of the chicken are browned and in the oven, add potatoes, soup mixture, and onion.
6. Set lid on the oven and transfer 17 coals to the lid, leaving 8 under the oven.
7. Cook for 30 minutes, then remove lid and add corn. Stir to cover the corn with soup mixture.
8. Return lid to the oven and bake for an additional 40 minutes or until the chicken reaches an internal temperature of 165°F. Refresh coals as needed. If potatoes are too firm, continue cooking until tender.

Michael Trdy
Cameron, Texas

3 tablespoons olive oil

5 pounds chicken thighs

½ teaspoon salt

1 teaspoon ground black pepper

1 (10.5-ounce) can condensed cream of chicken soup

1 (10.5-ounce) can condensed cheddar cheese soup

2 cups water

4 medium-size potatoes, peeled and thinly sliced

1 sweet onion, chopped

4 ears sweet corn on the cob, each cut into 3 pieces

Required equipment:
12-inch camp Dutch oven
Medium-size mixing bowl

KATAHDIN PORK AND CORNBREAD

Total servings: 12 to 14
Preparation time: 1 hour 30 minutes
Challenge level: Moderate

The camp Dutch oven's renowned multifunctionality is wonderfully demonstrated in this recipe from Jim Rausch, where the device begins as a fry pan, transitions to a pot, and ends as an oven. The complexity of the apricot preserves makes this a one-pot favorite!

2 tablespoons vegetable oil

2 pounds boneless pork

2 (1-ounce) packages taco seasoning mix

1 (8-ounce) jar salsa

1 (10-ounce) jar All Fruit apricot preserves

1 (28-ounce) can crushed tomatoes

1 (15-ounce) can kidney beans, rinsed and drained

1 (11-ounce) can corn

2 pounds Mexican blend shredded cheese

2 (8.5-ounce) packages Jiffy corn muffin mix

2 eggs

⅔ cup whole milk

Required equipment:
12-inch camp Dutch oven
2 1-gallon ziplock bags

Preparation at camp:

1. Warm oil in Dutch oven over 15 coals.
2. Chop pork into bite-size pieces.
3. Place meat into a 1-gallon ziplock bag along with taco seasoning. Seal bag and shake well, thoroughly coating meat with seasoning.
4. Fry coated pork in Dutch oven until meat is browned on the outside.
5. Add salsa, apricot preserves, crushed tomatoes, kidney beans, and corn to Dutch oven. Stir.
6. Cover oven and cook for 30 minutes. About 15 minutes after beginning this step, start a fresh batch of 25 coals.
7. After the 30 minutes is complete in step 6, add cheese to oven and stir well.
8. In a second 1-gallon ziplock bag, add corn muffin mix, eggs, and milk. Seal bag and knead contents until all large clumps disappear.
9. Snip a corner from bottom of ziplock bag and squeeze corn muffin batter evenly over top of the bubbling mixture in Dutch oven. Do not stir batter! Cover oven.
10. Place 8 fresh coals under the oven and 17 fresh coals on the lid.
11. Bake for 20 minutes or until top of cornbread is lightly browned and an inserted toothpick comes out clean.

Jim "Cinnamonboy" Rausch
Ellsworth, Maine

PINE BARREN CHICKEN CACCIATORE

Total servings: 12 to 14
Preparation time: 3 hours
Challenge level: Difficult

This recipe is one of our favorites. With a little thought and preparation, you can eat as well while camping as you do at home!

Required equipment:
12-inch camp Dutch oven
Cook pot

Preparation at camp:
1. Warm oil in Dutch oven over 20 coals.
2. Liberally cover the chicken thighs with adobo seasoning.
3. Brown chicken thighs on both sides in oven. Remove chicken from the oil and set aside.
4. Add bell pepper, onion, mushrooms, and garlic to the oil. Cook vegetables until tender.
5. Add chicken bouillon, water, crushed tomatoes, tomato sauce, bay leaf, oregano, basil, parsley, salt, and black pepper to the Dutch oven. Stir well.
6. Add chicken thighs, celery, and carrots to the oven. Stir again and place lid on Dutch oven.
7. Cooked for approximately 2 hours. Reduce number of coals as needed to bring sauce down to a simmer. It should not boil! Stir every 10 to 15 minutes while cooking, and be prepared to adjust or refresh coals as needed during cooking.
8. While the cacciatore is simmering, prepare pasta noodles in cook pot according to package directions.
9. Once the cacciatore is ready, remove bay leaf and serve over the pasta.

Tom Betancourt
Harrington Park, New Jersey

3 tablespoons extra-virgin olive oil

2 pounds skinless chicken thighs

Adobo seasoning to taste

1 green bell pepper, diced

1 onion, diced

8 ounces fresh mushrooms, sliced

2 cloves garlic, minced

1 chicken bouillon cube

1 cup water

1 (28-ounce) can crushed tomatoes

1 (29-ounce) can tomato sauce

1 bay leaf

½ tablespoon dried oregano

½ tablespoon dried basil

½ tablespoon dried parsley flakes

½ tablespoon salt

½ tablespoon ground black pepper

3 stalks celery, thinly sliced

3 carrots, thinly sliced

1 (16-ounce) package pasta noodles (your favorite)

MEDITERRANEAN CHICKEN

Total servings: 3 to 4
Preparation time: 30 minutes
Challenge level: Easy

5 tablespoons olive oil

1 pound chicken, skin removed, cut into bite-size pieces

2 lemons, juiced

1 tablespoon red wine vinegar

8 cloves garlic, minced

3 tablespoons herbes de Provence

2 medium-size red potatoes, chopped

1½ teaspoons salt

1 zucchini, chopped

1 red onion, cut into wedges

1 (6-ounce) jar sliced Kalamata olives, drained

Required equipment:
Medium-size standard Dutch oven

Preparation at camp:

1. Warm 1 tablespoon oil in a standard Dutch oven over medium heat.
2. Sear outside of chicken pieces in the hot oil.
3. Add remainder of ingredients to the oven, included remaining 4 tablespoons (¼ cup) olive oil. Stir.
4. Cook until all vegetables are tender and no pink remains in the chicken.

Christine and Tim Conners
Tucson, Arizona

ONE-POT THANKSGIVING

Total servings: 4
Preparation time: 45 minutes
Challenge level: Easy

This recipe comes from Peter Cabanillas, an outdoor skills instructor from Ellsworth, Maine.

Preparation at camp:

1. In a standard Dutch oven over medium heat, melt the butter, then sauté chicken until no pink remains.
2. Add the onion, celery, carrots, and corn. Stir and continue cooking until the carrots are soft.
3. Remove from heat. Add Craisins, walnuts, sage, and stuffing mix.
4. Stir well, cover, and allow to rest for a few minutes before serving.

Jim "Cinnamonboy" Rausch
Ellsworth, Maine

½ cup (1 standard stick) butter

2 boneless, skinless chicken breasts, cubed

1 small onion, chopped

2 stalks celery, chopped

2 carrots, peeled and sliced

1 (15-ounce) can corn, drained

4 ounces Craisins

½ cup chopped walnuts

1 tablespoon rubbed sage

1 (6-ounce) package Stove Top turkey stuffing mix

Required equipment:
Medium-size standard Dutch oven

KAHUNA CASSEROLE

Total servings: 6
Preparation time: 45 minutes
Challenge level: Moderate

1 pound lean ground beef

1 small onion, diced

2 tablespoons all-purpose flour

⅓ cup packed brown sugar

¼ teaspoon ginger powder

1 (20-ounce) can pineapple chunks, drained with juice reserved

1 (8-ounce) can crushed pineapple, drained with juice reserved

⅓ cup white vinegar

1 tablespoon soy sauce

1 green bell pepper, chopped

1 (8.5-ounce) package Barilla Ready Pasta penne noodles

Salt to taste

Required equipment:
Medium-size standard Dutch oven
Medium-size mixing bowl
Small mixing bowl

Preparation at camp:

1. In a standard Dutch oven over medium heat, brown ground beef and onion. Transfer beef and onion to a bowl.

2. In a small bowl, mix flour, brown sugar, and ginger powder.

3. Pour reserved pineapple juice, vinegar, and soy sauce into oven.

4. Stir in flour mixture until smooth. Heat to boiling.

5. Add bell pepper and pineapple to the oven. Continue to cook until heated through.

6. Add pasta and stir until noodles are coated with sauce.

7. Return cooked beef mixture to the oven and stir well. Salt to taste.

8. Cover, remove from heat, and allow to rest for a few minutes before serving.

Steve Deemer
Indiana, Pennsylvania

CINNAMONBOY CHILI

Total servings: 6
Preparation time: 1 hour
Challenge level: Easy

I was given the nickname "Cinnamonboy" because I added ground cinnamon to my coffee and to almost every other thing I cooked until my wife told me to knock it off.

Preparation at camp:
1. Brown meat in a standard Dutch oven over medium heat. A few minutes after adding the ground beef, add the onion and bell pepper too.
2. Once the pink is gone from the meat, stir in the tomatoes and bring to a simmer.
3. Add all the seasonings and cocoa powder. Continue over medium-low heat.
4. After about 10 to 20 minutes, stir in kidney beans.
5. Continue to cook for another 20 minutes or so, stirring occasionally.
6. Remove from heat and add salt to taste.

Option:
Ground turkey can be substituted for the ground beef, but add a little vegetable oil along with it to help this lean meat to brown.

Tip:
The longer this recipe simmers, the better it tastes!

Jim "Cinnamonboy" Rausch
Ellsworth, Maine

1 pound lean ground beef

1 onion, chopped

1 green bell pepper, chopped

1 (28-ounce) can crushed tomatoes

1 teaspoon chili powder

1 teaspoon ground cumin

1 teaspoon crushed red pepper

1 teaspoon garlic powder

1 teaspoon dried oregano

1 teaspoon dried basil

1 tablespoon ground cinnamon

1 teaspoon cocoa powder

1 (15-ounce) can kidney beans, rinsed and drained

Salt to taste

Required equipment:
Medium-size standard Dutch oven

INDIAN ISLAND ONION SOUP

Total servings: 6
Preparation time: 1 hour
Challenge level: Easy

We were camping at Indian Island Park in New York when the temperature dropped and I suddenly had a craving for hot soup! So I sautéed a Vidalia onion with some salt and pepper and threw a variation of this recipe together with what I had at camp. It tasted so good when the snow began to fall . . .

¼ cup (½ standard stick) butter

2 large Vidalia onions, sliced

2 cloves garlic, minced

1 teaspoon granulated sugar

½ teaspoon ground black pepper

1 (32-ounce) container beef broth

½ cup dry white wine

½ teaspoon salt

1 tablespoon dried thyme

2 handfuls Milton's crispy sea salt crackers

4 ounces shredded Gruyere cheese

Required equipment:
Medium-size standard Dutch oven

Preparation at camp:

1. Melt butter in a standard Dutch oven over medium heat.
2. Sauté the onions in the hot butter until caramelized.
3. Add garlic, sugar, black pepper, broth, wine, salt, and thyme to the oven. Stir well.
4. Cover, reduce heat, and simmer for about 30 minutes, stirring occasionally.
5. Uncover and evenly spread crackers over the soup. Top with cheese.
6. Cover, remove from heat, and allow soup to rest a few minutes while cheese melts.

Ken Spiegel
Medford, New York

FIRE TIPS

Total servings: 6
Preparation time: 2 hours
Challenge level: Easy

We were camping at our local favorite spot, Wompatuck State Park, where we gathered with a group of friends to spend a weekend in the woods by the fire. I began browning the meat for this recipe when I inadvertently added too much of the cayenne pepper and created an almost inedible meal. Inferno Tips! Lava Tips!! The meat ended up IN the fire after a few brave souls had a couple of bites. My wife still reminds me when I am cooking to not underestimate the generic brand cayenne.

Preparation at camp:

1. In a bowl, toss sirloin tips with flour.
2. Warm oil in a standard Dutch oven over medium heat.
3. Fry sirloin tips in hot oil until evenly browned on the outside.
4. Add all the remaining ingredients, except the rice, to the oven and stir until mixed.
5. Bring contents to a boil, then reduce temperature to low.
6. Cover and simmer for about 1½ hours until the meat becomes tender.
7. Add rice, stir well, cover, and allow to rest for about 10 minutes before serving.

Andy Mills
Bridgewater, Massachusetts

1½ pounds sirloin tips, cut into 1-inch cubes

¼ cup all-purpose flour

2 tablespoons olive oil

1½ cups ketchup

½ cup prepared mustard

½ cup brown sugar

2 cups water

1 teaspoon ground cayenne pepper

1 (8.5-ounce) package Ben's Original jasmine or basmati Ready Rice

Required equipment:
Medium-size standard Dutch oven
Medium-size mixing bowl

PICOS DE EUROPA PAELLA

Total servings: 6 to 8
Preparation time: 1 hour
Challenge level: Difficult

¼ cup olive oil

1 boneless, skinless chicken breast, cut into bite-size pieces

2 cloves garlic, minced

1 onion, diced

1 red bell pepper, chopped

1 yellow bell pepper, chopped

1 (14.5-ounce) can fire-roasted diced tomatoes

1 (14.5-ounce) can chicken broth

1 teaspoon paprika

½ teaspoon dried rosemary

½ teaspoon dried thyme

¼ teaspoon ground cumin

1 cup Spanish-style rice (arborio, bahia, bomba, calasparra, or senia)

13 ounces andouille sausage, cut into ¼-inch-thick rounds

1 (4-ounce) can peas, drained

¼ cup capers

2 pinches saffron

12 ounces raw shrimp, peeled, deveined, and thawed

1 lemon, cut into quarters

Salt and black pepper to taste

Required equipment:
Medium-size standard Dutch oven

Preparation at camp:
1. Warm oil in a standard Dutch oven over medium heat.
2. Fry chicken in hot oil until no pink remains.
3. Add garlic, onion, and peppers, and continue to cook until the vegetables are soft.
4. Add fire-roasted tomatoes, chicken broth, paprika, rosemary, thyme, cumin, rice, sausage, peas, capers, and saffron. Mix well.
5. Bring to a boil, then reduce heat to a simmer.
6. Lay shrimp over the rice. Cover.
7. Continue to cook for 20 minutes or until rice is plump and the shrimp is cooked through. Do not stir during this time!
8. Remove oven from heat and squeeze lemon juice over the mixture. Add salt and black pepper to taste.

Option:
A frozen seafood variety (a combination of calamari, whole-shell clams, mussels, etc.) can be used in place of the shrimp.

Brent Shull
Belleville, Illinois

BACKCOUNTRY BEEF STEW

Total servings: 6 to 8
Preparation time: 1 hour 30 minutes
Challenge level: Easy

My mom excelled at soups and stews. Once married, I took on the cooking of these dishes because I just knew what they should taste like. Drove my wife crazy because she measures everything and always follows a recipe. Me, not so much. I could never duplicate a recipe because who knew what was in there? Several of my recipes in this book are ones I first threw together during a camping trip using whatever I had on hand, and with just a vague idea of what I wanted to do!

Preparation at camp:
1. Place flour in a large ziplock bag. Add beef to the bag, seal, and shake to coat.
2. In a standard Dutch oven over medium heat, add oil and fry beef until browned on the outside. Add salt and black pepper to taste.
3. Add water to the oven, stir, and bring to a boil.
4. Add potatoes, carrots, bouillon cubes, and all remaining seasonings. Stir well.
5. Cook for about 45 minutes or until carrots and potatoes begin to soften.
6. Add celery and onion and cook for another 20 minutes or so. The longer the stew simmers, the better it tastes.

Option:
Gluten-free variation: This recipe works well with Bob's Red Mill gluten-free 1 to 1 Baking Flour.

Jim "Cinnamonboy" Rausch
Ellsworth, Maine

¼ cup all-purpose flour

1 pound stew beef, cubed

3 tablespoons olive oil

Salt and black pepper to taste

1 quart water

2 potatoes, cubed

3 carrots, peeled and sliced

2 cubes beef bouillon

¼ teaspoon dried basil

¼ teaspoon dried oregano

¼ teaspoon dried thyme

¼ teaspoon ground marjoram

¼ teaspoon garlic powder

3 stalks celery, thinly sliced

1 sweet onion, sliced

Required equipment:
Medium-size standard Dutch oven
1-gallon ziplock bag

WHITE MOUNTAIN CHILI

Total servings: 8
Preparation time: 30 minutes
Challenge level: Easy

It is amazing how delicious this recipe is for how easy it is to prepare.

2 tablespoons olive oil

1 pound ground turkey

1 onion, chopped

4 cloves garlic, minced

1 jalapeño pepper, seeded and chopped

2 (15-ounce) cans cannellini (white kidney) beans

1 (7-ounce) can diced green chilies

1 teaspoon salt

1½ teaspoons ground white pepper

1½ teaspoons ground cumin

1 pint heavy whipping cream

Optional toppings: shredded white cheddar cheese, chopped cilantro, crushed tortilla chips

Required equipment:
Medium-size standard Dutch oven

Preparation at camp:
1. Warm the oil in a standard Dutch oven over medium heat.
2. Fry the turkey, onion, and garlic in the hot oil.
3. Once the turkey is no longer pink, add all the remaining ingredients, except for the optional toppings. Mix well.
4. Continue cooking until the chili is heated through, about 10 minutes.
5. Serve in bowls, topped with your favorite optional toppings.

Christine and Tim Conners
Tucson, Arizona

HARDY WILD RICE SOUP

Total servings: 8
Preparation time: 45 minutes
Challenge level: Easy

An excellent recipe for a chilly evening!

Preparation at camp:
1. Melt butter in a standard Dutch oven over medium heat.
2. Cook onions in hot butter until soft, then blend in the flour.
3. Add water, evaporated milk, ham, carrots, potatoes, and rice. Stir until mixed.
4. Cover oven, bring to a boil, and continue to cook until vegetables are soft.
5. Stir in almonds, parsley flakes, and sherry.
6. Simmer uncovered for 5 minutes.

Edward Wollack
Clarksville, Maryland

¼ cup (½ standard stick) butter

1 onion, chopped

2 tablespoons all-purpose flour

5 cups water

1 (12-ounce) can evaporated milk

1 pound cooked ham, cubed

2 carrots, peeled and sliced

2 red potatoes, chopped

1 (6-ounce) package Ben's Original long grain and wild rice Original Recipe

¼ cup finely chopped almonds

1 tablespoon dried parsley flakes

1 tablespoon cooking sherry

Required equipment:
Medium-size standard Dutch oven

SPICY CHICKEN AND BLACK BEANS WITH RICE

Total servings: 8
Preparation time: 45 minutes (plus 1 hour for marinating)
Challenge level: Moderate

1 tablespoon chili powder

1 teaspoon crushed red pepper

1 tablespoon ground cumin

2 tablespoons olive oil

2 tablespoons white vinegar

2 tablespoons lemon juice

1 pound chicken, skin removed, cut into bite-size pieces

1 clove garlic, minced

1 small red onion, chopped

1 red bell pepper, chopped

1 (15-ounce) can corn, drained

1 (15-ounce) can black beans, rinsed and drained

1 (6.9-ounce) package Zatarain's yellow rice

3 cups water

2 cups shredded cheddar cheese

Optional toppings: sliced avocado, fresh cilantro, sour cream

Required equipment:
Medium-size standard Dutch oven
Medium-size mixing bowl

Preparation at camp:

1. In a bowl, mix together the chili powder, red pepper, cumin, olive oil, vinegar, and lemon juice.

2. Add chopped chicken to the bowl and toss to coat.

3. Cover bowl and store in a cool location for 1 hour, occasionally tossing to recoat the chicken.

4. Pour marinated chicken, including marinade, into a standard Dutch oven over medium heat.

5. Add garlic, onion, bell pepper, corn, black beans, rice, and water to the oven. Stir well.

6. Cook for about 30 minutes or until the rice is soft.

7. Stir in cheese, then serve with your favorite optional toppings.

Martha Charles
Rock Hill, South Carolina

WHITEWATER FISH CHOWDER

Total servings: 8
Preparation time: 1 hour
Challenge level: Moderate

Preparation at camp:
1. Melt butter in a standard Dutch oven over medium heat.
2. Fry fish in the hot butter until cooked through.
3. Add potatoes, celery, onion, jalapeños, garlic, and herbes de Provence. Stir well and sauté until potatoes are soft.
4. Add chicken broth, whipping cream, salt, and black pepper. Stir and simmer for another 20 minutes.
5. Stir in wine, then top with green onions.

Christine and Tim Conners
Tucson, Arizona

¼ cup (½ standard stick) butter

1½ pounds whitefish (cod, flounder, grouper, or trout), cut into pieces or shredded

3 potatoes, peeled and diced

3 stalks celery, chopped

1 onion, chopped

2 small jalapeño peppers, chopped

4 cloves garlic, minced

1 tablespoon herbes de Provence

1 (14.5-ounce) can chicken broth

1 pint heavy whipping cream

½ teaspoon salt

½ teaspoon ground black pepper

¼ cup dry white wine

3 green onions, chopped

Required equipment:
Medium-size standard Dutch oven

ISLA DE COZUMEL TACO SOUP

Total servings: 8 to 10
Preparation time: 30 minutes
Challenge level: Easy

1 tablespoon olive oil

1 pound ground turkey

1 large sweet onion, chopped

1 (1-ounce) package Pioneer chili seasoning

2 (15-ounce) cans kidney beans, rinsed and drained

2 tomatoes, chopped

1 bunch fresh cilantro, stemmed and chopped

2 small jalapeño peppers, chopped

1 (32-ounce) container chicken broth

Salt to taste

Toppings: crushed tortilla chips, lime juice, sour cream, sliced avocados, shredded cheese

Required equipment:
Medium-size standard Dutch oven

Preparation at camp:
1. Warm oil in a standard Dutch oven over medium heat.
2. Fry turkey until no longer pink.
3. Add onion, chili seasoning, beans, tomatoes, cilantro, jalapeños, and chicken broth. Stir well.
4. Simmer for about 15 minutes.
5. Serve in bowls with your favorite toppings.

Emily Kochetta
Statesboro, Georgia

FINGER LICKIN' GOOD CHICKEN TETRAZZINI

Total servings: 8 to 10
Preparation time: 45 minutes
Challenge level: Moderate

When our Scout troop tries a new recipe on a campout, the adults watch the Scouts' reactions, then ask, "Well? Do we add it to our list of favorites?" The first time we prepared this dish, the answer was a resounding "Yes!" At the next troop meeting, three parents asked for the recipe because their Scouts raved about it at home. Later, the same parents reported that it was one of the best meals they ever had. Truly is finger lickin' good!

Preparation at camp:

1. In a standard Dutch oven over medium heat, melt butter then sauté onion and celery until tender.
2. Evenly arrange chicken over the vegetables. Add fettuccine noodles in a layer over chicken.
3. In a large bowl, combine soup, broth, lemon juice, black pepper, and nutmeg. Mix well, then pour the liquid over the fettuccine.
4. Add water as needed to just cover the fettuccine.
5. Sprinkle mushrooms over the noodles.
6. Cover oven, increase the heat, and bring to a boil.
7. Stir then reduce heat to a simmer, stirring occasionally.
8. Cook for about 20 minutes or until fettucini is tender.
9. Garnish with Parmesan cheese and paprika.

Greg Woodside
Chalfont, Pennsylvania

3 tablespoons butter

1 medium-size onion, chopped

4 stalks celery, chopped

2 pounds skinless chicken breast, cut into small cubes

12 ounces fettuccine pasta, broken in half

1 (10.5-ounce) can condensed cream of mushroom soup

1 (14.5-ounce) can chicken broth

1 teaspoon lemon juice

¼ teaspoon ground black pepper

1 pinch ground nutmeg

Water, as needed to just cover noodles

8 ounces fresh mushrooms, sliced

1 cup grated Parmesan cheese

Paprika to taste

Required equipment:
Medium-size standard Dutch oven
Large mixing bowl

CHILL-OUT JAMBALAYA

Total servings: 8 to 10
Preparation time: 1 hour 15 minutes
Challenge level: Moderate

2 tablespoons olive oil

1 pound chicken, skin removed, cut into bite-size pieces

13 ounces smoked andouille or kielbasa sausage, chopped

1 onion, chopped

4 cloves garlic, minced

1 green bell pepper, chopped

4 scallions, chopped

2 stalks celery, chopped

1 (14.5-ounce) can diced tomatoes

1 (14.5-ounce) can chicken broth

2 tablespoons Worcestershire sauce

½ teaspoon dried thyme

¼ teaspoon ground cayenne pepper

1 tablespoon Old Bay seasoning

2 cups long grain rice

1 (12-ounce) package raw shrimp, peeled, deveined, and thawed

Salt to taste

Required equipment:
Medium-size standard Dutch oven

Preparation at camp:

1. Warm oil over medium heat in a standard Dutch oven.

2. Add chicken pieces to the hot oil. About 5 minutes later, add the sausage, onion, garlic, bell pepper, scallions, and celery.

3. Continue cooking until the chicken is no longer pink and the vegetables have softened, about 20 minutes.

4. Stir in tomatoes and broth.

5. Season with Worcestershire sauce, thyme, cayenne, and Old Bay. Stir well.

6. Increase heat, bring to a boil, and add the rice.

7. Cover oven and cook for about 35 minutes or until the rice is cooked through, stirring occasionally. Refresh coals as needed.

8. Reduce heat, add shrimp, and continue cooking until the shrimp is no longer pink. Add salt to taste and serve.

Jim "Cinnamonboy" Rausch
Ellsworth, Maine

MULE-SKINNER BEANS

Total servings: 10 to 12
Preparation time: 4 hours 15 minutes
Challenge level: Moderate

I invented this recipe while in optometry school during a fit of hunger. The olive oil eventually informs the flavor of the beans and is the secret ingredient that makes people say ooh and aah!

Preparation at camp:

1. In a standard Dutch oven, combine water, pinto beans, barley, olive oil, ham hock, jalapeños, and salt. Stir and cover.
2. Cook over medium heat for at least 3 hours. Replenish water while cooking if the evaporation is high.
3. Add bell pepper and ground black pepper to taste, then cook for about 1 more hour.
4. Add mushrooms, zucchini, tomatoes, garlic, and cilantro and cook for about 15 more minutes, giving time for the just-added vegetables to soften.
5. Move oven from heat, remove ham hock from oven, then shred any remaining meat bits off the bone.
6. Add the shredded meat back to the pot and toss the bone away. Stir and serve.

Paul Gooch
St. George, Utah

3 quarts water

1 cup dried pinto beans

1 cup pearled barley

¾ cup extra-virgin olive oil

1 ham hock

2 jalapeño peppers, chopped

2 teaspoons salt

1 green bell pepper, chopped

Ground black pepper to taste

8 ounces fresh mushrooms, chopped

1 small zucchini, chopped

2 tomatoes, chopped

4 cloves garlic, minced

1 bunch fresh cilantro, stemmed and chopped

Required equipment:
Medium-size standard Dutch oven

HAWAIIAN-STYLE TERIYAKI STIR FRY

Total servings: 2
Preparation time: 45 minutes
Challenge level: Easy

I grew up in Hawaii, where one of my favorite dishes was teriyaki stir fry. The key is the sauce, which, in Hawaii, tends to be thicker and sweeter than traditional teriyaki. Soy Vay makes a good thick version, and I've included that in the ingredients here. ~ Christine

3 tablespoons vegetable oil

2 boneless, skinless chicken breasts, cubed

1 cup Soy Vay Veri Veri teriyaki sauce

2 cups colorful chopped blend of any of these vegetables: bell pepper, fresh garlic, carrots, broccoli, cauliflower, baby bok choy, or sweet onion

Required equipment:
Medium-size skillet

Preparation at camp:
1. Warm oil in skillet over high heat.
2. Cook the chicken until no longer pink.
3. Add the teriyaki sauce to the pan along with your favorite chopped vegetables.
4. Continue stirring until vegetables are soft.

Options:
Prepare your own Hawaiian teriyaki sauce by combining soy sauce, crushed fresh garlic, grated ginger, and sugar to taste. Serve the stir fry as is or over rice. One pound of cubed extra-firm tofu can be substituted for the chicken to make a vegan version of this recipe.

Christine and Tim Conners
Tucson, Arizona

COCONUT CURRY CHICKEN

Total servings: 4
Preparation time: 45 minutes
Challenge level: Easy

Preparation at camp:

1. Warm oil in a skillet over medium heat.
2. Fry chicken, onion, and garlic until chicken is fully cooked with no pink remaining.
3. Add curry powder, carrots, bell pepper, sweet potato, and coconut milk. Stir well.
4. Simmer until all vegetables are cooked through. Add salt and black pepper to taste.
5. Add rice and cook for a few more minutes, stirring until the rice is broken up and warmed through.

Christine and Tim Conners
Tucson, Arizona

2 tablespoons olive oil

1 boneless, skinless chicken breast, cut into bite-size pieces

1 sweet onion, chopped

2 cloves garlic, minced

2 tablespoons curry powder

2 medium-size carrots, peeled and chopped

1 green bell pepper, chopped

1 small sweet potato, peeled and chopped

1 (14-ounce) can coconut milk

Salt and black pepper to taste

1 (8.8-ounce) package Ben's Original jasmine Ready Rice

Required equipment:
Medium-size skillet

CUBAN-STYLE PICADILLO

Total servings: 4
Preparation time: 45 minutes
Challenge level: Easy

Picadillo is a type of hash common throughout Latin America. Roughly translated from Spanish, it means "little minced meat." Every nationality has its own version. In Mexico, they might add cinnamon and almonds and use it as a filling for chiles rellenos, tacos, or burritos, while Cubans might add cumin, bell peppers, green olives, or capers and serve it with rice and black beans. Although the combination of raisins and olives may seem wild, give it a try. You'll probably be pleasantly surprised by the taste!

1 pound ground beef

2 tablespoons white vinegar

1 teaspoon minced garlic

1 teaspoon ground cumin

1 tablespoon vegetable oil

1 onion, chopped

1 red bell pepper, chopped

1 (8-ounce) can tomato sauce

¼ cup raisins

¼ cup sliced green olives

1 (8.8-ounce) package Ben's Original whole grain brown Ready Rice

Salt and black pepper to taste

Required equipment:
Large skillet
Medium-size mixing bowl

Preparation at camp:

1. Thoroughly mix ground beef, vinegar, garlic, and cumin in a bowl. Cover meat mixture and let rest for about 15 minutes.
2. Warm oil over medium heat in a skillet
3. Sauté onion and bell pepper in the hot oil.
4. Once onion and pepper are soft, add the marinated ground beef and cook until the pink disappears.
5. Stir in tomato sauce, raisins, olives, and rice and simmer for 5 to 10 minutes.
6. Add salt and pepper to taste.

Pat Brown
Los Osos, California

ITALIAN VEGETABLE SKILLET DINNER

Total servings: 6
Preparation time: 45 minutes
Challenge level: Easy

Preparation at camp:

1. In a skillet over medium heat, brown the ground beef along with onion and bell pepper. Set ground beef mixture aside.
2. Cook potatoes with garlic until potatoes soften and begin to brown. Stir frequently.
3. Reduce heat and return browned meat to skillet. Mix thoroughly.
4. Stir in diced tomatoes and vegetable soup, then add basil, oregano, and chili powder.
5. Increase heat, bringing contents to a boil briefly, then reduce heat to medium-low and stir in celery flakes.
6. Simmer for about 10 minutes.
7. Remove from heat, sprinkle Parmesan cheese over top, and add salt to taste.

Steve Deemer
Indiana, Pennsylvania

1 pound ground beef

1 small onion, chopped

1 green bell pepper, chopped

2 medium-size potatoes, peeled and diced

2 cloves garlic, minced

1 (14.5-ounce) can diced tomatoes

1 (18-ounce) can ready-to-eat vegetable soup

1 tablespoon dried basil

1 tablespoon dried oregano

½ teaspoon chili powder

½ teaspoon dried celery flakes

Grated Parmesan cheese to taste

Salt to taste

Required equipment:
Large skillet

POTATO PILLOWS IN HEAVENLY SAUSAGE SAUCE

Total servings: 6
Preparation time: 45 minutes
Challenge level: Easy

1 pound ground turkey sausage

3 tablespoons olive oil

1 (16-ounce) package frozen pierogies, thawed

1 (14-ounce) jar pizza sauce

1 (10-ounce) can diced tomatoes with green chilies

1 teaspoon paprika

1 teaspoon onion powder

1 teaspoon garlic powder

1 teaspoon granulated sugar

1 small sweet onion, diced

1 stalk celery, diced

1 green bell pepper, diced

Crushed red pepper to taste

Required equipment:
Large skillet
Medium-size mixing bowl

Preparation at camp:
1. Fry turkey in a skillet over medium heat until no longer pink. Set aside in a bowl.
2. Add olive oil to the pan. Brown the pierogies in oil until lightly browned on the outside.
3. Return cooked turkey to the pan and add remainder of ingredients.
4. Simmer for about 20 minutes or until the vegetables are soft.

Ken Spiegel
Medford, New York

ALL THE FIXIN'S BURGERS!

Total servings: 8
Preparation time: 45 minutes
Challenge level: Moderate

The fixin's are inside the burger!

Preparation at camp:

1. In a bowl and using your hands, mix together ground beef, gravy, tomatoes, onions, mushrooms, and cheese. Be prepared for a sticky mess!
2. Form meat mixture into 8 patties.
3. Fry burgers in a well-greased skillet over medium heat until cooked through.
4. Serve on buns with your favorite toppings.

Tips:

Important: This style of burger will cook more slowly than regular burgers because of all the extra ingredients, and the burgers will be more inclined to crumble. Cook patiently over a lower, steady heat, and flip only once!

Harold Robinson
Quarryville, Pennsylvania

2 pounds lean ground beef

¾ cup Heinz Home Style beef gravy

½ cup diced tomatoes

½ cup diced onions

½ cup diced fresh mushrooms

8 ounces shredded cheese (your choice)

8 hamburger buns

Toppings: cheese slices, sliced tomatoes, sliced onions, lettuce, ketchup, mayonnaise, yellow mustard

Required equipment:

Large skillet
Large mixing bowl

Side Dishes

ROSEMARY AND GARLIC ROASTED POTATOES

Total servings: 4
Preparation time: 1 hour 15 minutes
Challenge level: Easy

V

1 pound red new potatoes (about 6 total)

¼ cup olive oil

2 fresh rosemary sprigs

5 cloves garlic, thinly sliced

½ teaspoon dried oregano

½ teaspoon dried basil

½ teaspoon onion powder

Salt and black pepper to taste

Required equipment:
10-inch camp Dutch oven

Preparation at camp:

1. Preheat Dutch oven over 21 coals.
2. Clean potatoes. Dry well, then cut into 6 to 8 wedges each.
3. Bring oil to a simmer in the hot oven.
4. Carefully add potatoes to the oven along with rosemary sprigs, garlic, oregano, basil, and onion powder.
5. Carefully stir to coat all the ingredients in oil, then season generously with salt and black pepper.
6. Cover Dutch oven and move all coals to the lid to form a broiler.
7. Stir occasionally so that that the contents don't burn. The dish is ready once potatoes are a golden brown, about 35 minutes.
8. Remove rosemary sprigs. Stir to coat potatoes with oil.

Option:
For a lacto-ovo vegetarian option, serve with sour cream and shredded Parmesan cheese.

Jason Cagle
Jacksonville, Florida

ITALIAN CHEESE BOMBS

V-LO

Total servings: 4 to 8
Preparation time: 45 minutes
Challenge level: Moderate

Preparation at camp:
1. Prepare 21 coals for the Dutch oven.
2. Slice mozzarella cheese block into 16 cubes.
3. Cut each of the 8 dough biscuits in half to form 16 flat disks.
4. One disk at a time, fold the dough around a piece of cheese and roll the dough between your palms to form a ball.
5. Add olive oil to a bowl.
6. In a second bowl, combine Parmesan cheese and Italian seasoning.
7. Dip one side of each dough ball in olive oil then in the seasoning mix.
8. Set dough balls in Dutch oven side-by-side.
9. Using 14 coals on the lid and 7 coals under the oven, bake cheese balls for 20 to 30 minutes or until tops turn a light golden brown.
10. Meanwhile, briefly warm marinara sauce in a small pot resting on the coals.
11. Serve, dipping cheese bombs in the marinara sauce.

Options:
For a nonvegetarian option, add salami or pepperoni slices to the dough disks along with the cheese cubes in step 4.

Jim "Cinnamonboy" Rausch
Ellsworth, Maine

1 (8-ounce) block mozzarella cheese

1 (16-ounce) container refrigerated biscuit dough

2 tablespoons olive oil

¼ cup grated Parmesan cheese

¼ cup Italian seasoning blend

1 small jar marinara sauce

Required equipment:
10-inch camp Dutch oven
Small cook pot
2 small mixing bowls

COWBOY BOB'S JALAPEÑO BITES

Total servings: 6 to 8
Preparation time: 45 minutes
Challenge level: Easy

1 (8-ounce) package
cream cheese, softened

8 ounces (about 2 cups)
grated Parmesan cheese

6 small jalapeño
peppers, seeded and
chopped

¼ pound precooked
sausage, chopped into
small pieces

1 large egg, beaten

Johnny's seasoning
salt or Log Cabin Grub
seasoning to taste

3 cups dry plain bread
crumbs

Required equipment:
12-inch camp Dutch
oven
Medium-size mixing
bowl

Preparation at camp:

1. Preheat Dutch oven using 17 coals on the lid
   and 8 coals under the oven.

2. In a bowl, mix cream cheese, Parmesan
   cheese, jalapeños, sausage, egg, and
   seasoning to form a paste.

3. Shape into balls using a heaping ½
   tablespoon of paste for each.

4. Roll the balls in the bread crumbs on a
   clean surface.

5. Place half of the balls inside the Dutch
   oven and bake for 10 to 15 minutes or until
   golden brown. Repeat with the second
   batch.

6. Serve warm.

Robert "Cowboy Bob" Dowdy
Great Falls, Montana

SWEET POTATO BAKE

Total servings: 6 to 8
Preparation time: 1 hour
Challenge level: Easy

Preparation at camp:

1. Prepare 21 coals for the Dutch oven.
2. In a bowl, combine sweet potatoes, butter, pecans, sugar, and salt. Stir well.
3. Pour sweet potato mixture into a parchment-lined Dutch oven, then evenly distribute marshmallows over the top.
4. Using 14 coals on top of the oven and 7 coals underneath, bake for 40 minutes or until marshmallows melt and potatoes are heated through.
5. Allow to cool for a few minutes before serving.

Christine and Tim Conners
Tucson, Arizona

1 (29-ounce) can sweet potatoes, drained and mashed

¼ cup (½ standard stick) butter, softened

½ cup chopped pecans

½ cup brown sugar

⅛ teaspoon salt

16 regular-size marshmallows, sliced in half

Required equipment:
10-inch camp Dutch oven
Large mixing bowl
Parchment paper

DEEP SEA CRABBY ROLLS

Total servings: 6 to 8
Preparation time: 1 hour 15 minutes
Challenge level: Moderate

3 cups self-rising flour

2 tablespoons granulated sugar

1⅛ cups whole milk

1 (8-ounce) package cream cheese, softened

8 ounces real crabmeat

3 cloves garlic, minced

4 green onions, chopped

½ teaspoon ground black pepper

1 teaspoon Worcestershire sauce

½ teaspoon blackened seasoning

1 teaspoon lemon juice

Required equipment:
12-inch camp Dutch oven
Large mixing bowl
Rolling pin or cylindrical water bottle
Parchment paper

Preparation at camp:

1. Prepare 23 coals for the Dutch oven.
2. While coals are heating, combine flour, sugar, and milk in a bowl. Knead well with hands.
3. Set dough on a lightly floured surface and, using a rolling pin or cylindrical water bottle, roll dough flat into a rectangle, about 8 by 12 inches in size.
4. Combine cream cheese, crabmeat, garlic, onions, black pepper, Worcestershire sauce, blackened seasoning, and lemon juice in the bowl. Mix well.
5. Spread crab filling evenly over top of the dough.
6. Roll up dough as you would a sleeping bag, from long side to long side. You'll be creating a cylinder about 12 inches long.
7. Slice the cylinder into 1-inch-thick rolls.
8. Lay rolls side-by-side in a parchment-lined 12-inch Dutch oven.
9. Bake using 16 coals on top of the oven and 7 coals underneath for about 45 minutes, until rolls become firm. Refresh coals if necessary.

Christine and Tim Conners
Tucson, Arizona

BLUE CHEESE POTATO SALAD

Total servings: 6 to 8
Preparation time: 1 hour 30 minutes
Challenge level: Moderate

V-LO

Preparation at camp:
1. Prepare 23 coals for the Dutch oven.
2. Clean potatoes, then wipe with oil and poke potatoes aggressively with a fork.
3. Bake potatoes in Dutch oven using 16 coals on top and 7 coals under the oven for about 1 hour or until potatoes are soft.
4. Remove potatoes from oven. Once cooled enough to work with, cut into cubes.
5. Return potatoes to oven. Stir in celery, dill weed, blue cheese dressing, onions, and eggs.
6. Add salt and pepper to taste.

Christine and Tim Conners
Tucson, Arizona

4 large red potatoes

1 tablespoon olive oil

1 stalk celery, chopped

1 teaspoon dried dill weed

¾ cup chunky blue cheese dressing

2 green onions, chopped

3 precooked hard-boiled eggs, chopped into pieces

Salt and black pepper to taste

Required equipment:
10-inch camp Dutch oven

BERLINER BACON DATE WRAPS

Total servings: 8
Preparation time: 45 minutes
Challenge level: Easy

12 slices bacon

24 Medjool dates, seeds removed

½ cup (1 standard stick) butter, softened

¾ cup honey

Required equipment:
10-inch camp Dutch oven
Small mixing bowl

Preparation at camp:
1. Prepare 21 coals for the Dutch oven.
2. Cut each slice of bacon in half.
3. Wrap a date in each of the bacon halves.
4. As each date is wrapped, set side-by-side in the Dutch oven.
5. Combine butter and honey in a bowl and pour over the dates.
6. Bake using 14 coals on the lid and 7 coals under the oven for about 25 minutes.

Options:
Not a fan of dates? Try goat cheese or fried chicken liver instead!

Michael Kaiserauer
Berlin, Germany

CORN MUSH CASSEROLE

Total servings: 8 to 10
Preparation time: 1 hour
Challenge level: Easy

Preparation at camp:

1. Melt ½ cup (1 standard stick) butter in Dutch oven over 23 coals. Remove oven from coals as soon as butter is fully melted.
2. Add whole-kernel corn, creamed corn, eggs, muffin mix, and sour cream to oven. Stir well.
3. Moving 16 coals to the lid and leaving 7 under the oven, bake for about 40 minutes, until the top is a light golden brown and an inserted knife comes out clean.
4. Mix ¼ cup (½ standard stick) butter and honey in a small bowl to make the topping.
5. Serve casserole with the topping.

Carl Laub
Arlington Heights, Illinois

¾ cup (1½ standard sticks) butter, softened

1 (15.25-ounce) can whole-kernel corn

1 (14.75-ounce) can creamed corn

2 eggs

1 (8.5-ounce) package Jiffy corn muffin mix

1 cup sour cream

2 tablespoons honey

Required equipment:
10-inch camp Dutch oven
Small mixing bowl

BIG RIVER BACON N' CHEESE TATERS

Total servings: 8 to 10
Preparation time: 1 hour 30 minutes
Challenge level: Moderate

1 pound bacon, chopped

1 sweet onion, diced

2 jalapeño peppers, seeded and chopped

8 medium-size red new potatoes, chopped

1 (8-ounce) package cream cheese, softened

1 (8-ounce) package shredded Monterey Jack cheese

Salt and black pepper to taste

Required equipment:
10-inch camp Dutch oven

Preparation at camp:

1. Preheat Dutch oven over 21 coals.
2. Brown bacon in the oven.
3. Add onion and jalapeños, then cook for 5 minutes.
4. Add chopped potatoes. Stir well.
5. Move 14 coals to the lid and leave 7 coals under the oven. Cook for another 5 minutes with lid on.
6. Add cream cheese and half of the shredded cheese to the oven. Stir well.
7. Bake for an additional 45 minutes, stirring every 15 minutes.
8. Cover with remainder of the cheese and allow to melt across the top.
9. Serve, adding salt and black pepper to taste.

Robert "Cowboy Bob" Dowdy
Great Falls, Montana

ALPINE BAKED BEANS

Total servings: 12 to 14
Preparation time: 1 hour
Challenge level: Easy

Preparation at camp:

1. Combine all of the ingredients in a standard Dutch oven.
2. Cook over medium heat for about 40 minutes, stirring periodically. Add additional water in small quantities if beans appear too thick.
3. Remove bay leaf before serving.

Mark Case, Sr.
Randleman, North Carolina

2 (29-ounce) cans great northern beans, rinsed and drained

1 small onion, chopped

1 bay leaf

1 cup packed brown sugar

½ cup molasses

1 pound cooked ham or Canadian bacon, chopped into small pieces

½ tablespoon ground mustard

¼ cup Worcestershire sauce

½ teaspoon ground ginger

½ teaspoon ground cloves

1 teaspoon salt

1 cup water

Required equipment:
Medium-size standard Dutch oven

CAST IRON MEXICAN CORN

V-LO

Total servings: 4 to 6
Preparation time: 30 minutes
Challenge level: Easy

The first time we tried Mexican corn on the cob, we fell in love with it! This is a simple knock-off for cast iron cooking, a unique and delicious side dish to enhance just about any main course.

2 tablespoons vegetable oil

1 (16-ounce) package frozen sweet corn, thawed

2 small jalapeño peppers, diced

2 teaspoons chili powder

½ cup queso fresco

½ cup crema Mexicana

1 lime

¼ cup chopped fresh cilantro

Required equipment:
Large skillet

Preparation at camp:
1. In a skillet over medium-high heat, combine oil, corn, jalapeños, and chili powder.
2. Heat and toss until corn becomes a golden brown, about 10 minutes.
3. Remove from heat and allow to sit for about 10 minutes.
4. Add queso fresco, Mexican crema, the juice of the lime, and cilantro.
5. Toss and serve.

Christine and Tim Conners
Tucson, Arizona

THYME FOR GREEN BEANS

Total servings: 4 to 6
Preparation time: 45 minutes
Challenge level: Easy

V

Preparation at camp:
1. Trim and rinse green beans.
2. Add beans to skillet with water and garlic salt.
3. Bring to a boil over medium-high heat. Continue to cook until nearly all water has evaporated, stirring occasionally.
4. Reduce heat to medium. Add oil to the pan along with thyme, celery seed, and cayenne pepper. Stir to coat the green beans.
5. Continue to cook until beans begin to blacken, about 20 minutes.
6. Add black pepper to taste.

Tip:
Boiling off the water before adding the oil helps to precook the green beans without turning them soft and mushy.

Christine and Tim Conners
Tucson, Arizona

1 pound fresh green beans
¼ cup water
¼ teaspoon garlic salt
2 tablespoons olive oil
1 teaspoon dried thyme
½ teaspoon celery seed
1 pinch ground cayenne pepper
Ground black pepper to taste

Required equipment:
Medium-size skillet

Breads

RIPPED CORN BREAD

Total servings: 6
Preparation time: 45 minutes
Challenge level: Easy

Yeah, you read that correctly. Ripped.

1 tablespoon vegetable oil

1 (8.5-ounce) package Jiffy corn muffin mix

1 (14.75-ounce) can creamed corn

1 egg

1 jalapeño pepper, chopped

¼ cup sour cream

¼ cup chili powder

Required equipment:
10-inch camp Dutch oven
Medium-size mixing bowl

Preparation at camp:
1. Prepare 21 coals for the Dutch oven.
2. Add oil to Dutch oven.
3. In a bowl, combine muffin mix, creamed corn, egg, jalapeño, sour cream, and chili powder. Mix well.
4. Pour batter into oven and bake using 14 coals on the lid and 7 coals under the oven for about 30 minutes or until a knife comes out clean.

Option:
Goes great as a side with your favorite chili or stew!

Christine and Tim Conners
Tucson, Arizona

HAWAIIAN SUN ROLLS

Total servings: 6 to 8
Preparation time: 1 hour
Challenge level: Moderate

V-LO

Growing up in Hawaii, we ate a lot of the Hawaiian bread rolls so prevalent today. This recipe re-creates the magic of those rolls from home. ~ Christine

Preparation at camp:
1. Prepare 21 coals for the Dutch oven.
2. In a bowl, combine yeast, warm water, and 1 teaspoon brown sugar. Stir briefly and allow to rest for 10 minutes.
3. Add pineapple juice, ⅓ cup brown sugar, 4 tablespoons butter, eggs, salt, and vanilla extract to the bowl. Stir.
4. Approximately 1 cup at a time, add flour to the bowl, mixing well after each cup.
5. Form 1 dozen hand-size dough balls; that is, each ball should roughly fit within an adult fist.
6. Spread remaining 2 tablespoons of butter over the bottom of a parchment-lined Dutch oven.
7. Place dough balls on buttered lining in oven.
8. Using 14 coals on the lid and 7 coals under the oven, bake for about 30 minutes or until the tops of the rolls are a light golden brown.

Options:
For an extra treat, spread a mixture of honey and softened butter on the parchment-lined bottom of the oven before adding dough. Or try the rolls as buns for mini-burgers!

Christine and Tim Conners
Tucson, Arizona

1 (0.25-ounce) package rapid-rise yeast

2 tablespoons warm water

1 teaspoon plus ⅓ cup packed brown sugar

¾ cup pineapple juice, room temperature

6 tablespoons butter, softened

2 eggs

1 teaspoon salt

1 teaspoon vanilla extract

3½ cups all-purpose flour

Required equipment:
10-inch camp Dutch oven
Large mixing bowl
Parchment paper

HONEY SWEET ROLLS

V-LO

Total servings: 8
Preparation time: 2 hours
Challenge level: Moderate

9 tablespoons butter, softened

2 tablespoons plus ½ cup honey

1 cup whole milk, lukewarm

1 (0.25-ounce) package rapid-rise yeast

1 large egg

4 cups all-purpose flour

1 teaspoon salt

Required equipment:
10-inch camp Dutch oven
2 small mixing bowls
Large mixing bowl
Parchment paper

Preparation at camp:

1. In a small bowl, combine 4 tablespoons butter and 2 tablespoons honey. Cover and set aside.
2. In a second small bowl, combine milk, ½ cup honey, and yeast. Let rest until liquid begins to bubble.
3. In a large bowl, combine 4 tablespoons butter, egg, flour, and salt. Stir well.
4. Slowly add milk mixture to flour mixture while kneading the dough. If the dough seems too dry, add some water in very small quantities at a time while continuing to knead.
5. Form dough into a large ball in the bowl, then cover bowl with a towel. Allow dough to rise for about 1 hour in a warm location.
6. Prepare 23 coals for the Dutch oven.
7. Line Dutch oven with parchment paper.
8. Break the dough apart and roll with hands into 1 dozen balls, setting the balls side-by-side in the oven.
9. Brush 1 tablespoon softened butter over the tops of the rolls.
10. Bake using 16 coals on the lid and 7 coals under the oven for 25 minutes or until rolls are a light golden brown on top.
11. Serve with the honey butter.

Tips:
If you don't have parchment paper in your cooking kit, greased aluminum foil can be used instead. Also, the rolls can be punched out of flattened dough using a biscuit cutter, either purchased or by improvising using a clean can.

Christine and Tim Conners
Tucson, Arizona

MACADAMIA NUT BANANA BREAD

V-LO

Total servings: 8 to 10
Preparation time: 1 hour 15 minutes
Challenge level: Easy

Preparation at camp:

1. Prepare 25 coals for the Dutch oven.
2. Line Dutch oven with parchment paper.
3. Combine butter, bananas, eggs, and vanilla extract in a medium-size bowl. Mix well.
4. In a large bowl, whisk together the flour, sugar, baking soda, salt, and nuts.
5. Add the wet ingredients to the bowl with the dry ingredients and mix well.
6. Pour batter into oven.
7. Place 17 coals on the lid of the oven and 8 coals underneath.
8. Bake for about 45 to 55 minutes or until an inserted knife comes out clean.

Christine and Tim Conners
Tucson, Arizona

½ cup (1 standard stick) butter, softened

3 ripe bananas, mashed

2 eggs

1 teaspoon vanilla extract

2 cups unbleached flour

1 cup brown sugar

1 teaspoon baking soda

½ teaspoon salt

1 cup chopped macadamia nuts

Required equipment:
12-inch camp Dutch oven
Medium-size mixing bowl
Large mixing bowl
Parchment paper

JALAPEÑO CHEDDAR BEER BREAD

Total servings: 8 to 10
Preparation time: 1 hour 30 minutes
Challenge level: Moderate

V-LO

3½ cups all-purpose flour

1 tablespoon baking powder

3 tablespoons granulated sugar

1½ teaspoons salt

1 jalapeño pepper, chopped

1 cup shredded smoked cheddar cheese

2 (12-ounce) cans lager beer

1 egg, beaten

Required equipment:
12-inch camp Dutch oven
Large mixing bowl
Wire rack or grate

Preparation at camp:

1. Preheat Dutch oven using 18 coals on the lid and 9 coals under the oven.
2. Combine flour, baking powder, sugar, and salt in a bowl.
3. Add jalapeño and cheese to the bowl and mix well.
4. Add contents from *one* can of beer to the bowl. Mix until ingredients are just combined. Don't overwork the dough.
5. Turn dough onto a lightly floured surface. Knead quickly to form a ball.
6. Place dough ball in the hot Dutch oven.
7. Slit an X across the top of the dough ball using a serrated or very sharp knife, then quickly brush the dough ball with beaten egg.
8. Return lid to oven and bake until golden brown, about 45 minutes. Refresh coals if necessary.
9. Transfer bread to a wire rack or grate to cool.
10. Now is the time for that extra beer. Cook's treat!

Tip:
Don't have a cooking brush? Use the corner of a folded paper towel instead.

Robert "Cowboy Bob" Dowdy
Great Falls, Montana

MOM'S ZUCCHINI BREAD

Total servings: 10 to 12
Preparation time: 1 hour 45 minutes
Challenge level: Easy

V-LO

This fantastic recipe was handed down from Tim's mom and is one of the most replicated recipes throughout the Conners family. Mom would bake big batches of loaves when her grandkids came to visit. Always a treat, we've adapted it here for the joy of all!

Preparation at camp:
1. Prepare 19 coals for the Dutch oven.
2. In a bowl, thoroughly mix all the ingredients together.
3. Pour batter into a parchment-lined Dutch oven.
4. Bake for 1 hour 20 minutes to 1 hour 30 minutes using 13 coals on the lid and 6 coals under the oven, refreshing coals as needed. Bread is ready once an inserted knife comes out clean.

Christine and Tim Conners
Tucson, Arizona

3 eggs

1 cup vegetable oil

2 cups shredded and finely chopped zucchini

1 teaspoon baking soda

½ teaspoon baking powder

1 teaspoon pumpkin pie spice

1 teaspoon ground cinnamon

1 teaspoon salt

1 tablespoon vanilla extract

2 cups granulated sugar

3 cups all-purpose flour

1 cup chopped nuts (your favorite)

Required equipment:
10-inch camp Dutch oven
Large mixing bowl
Parchment paper

EASY JOURNEY CAKES

Total servings: 3 to 4
Preparation time: 30 minutes
Challenge level: Easy

It's said that New England settlers learned variations of this recipe from the Pawtuxet Native Americans, a skill that saved the settlers from starvation. This flat cornbread has gone by many different names over the years, including johnnycake, Shawnee cake, and hoecake. But our favorite name is "journey cake" because original versions were well-suited for long journeys.

1 (8.5-ounce) package Jiffy corn muffin mix

1 egg

⅓ cup whole milk

2 tablespoons butter

Honey to taste

Required equipment:
Medium-size skillet
Quart-size ziplock bag

Preparation at camp:
1. In a quart-size ziplock bag, combine muffin mix, egg, and milk. Seal bag and knead the contents until lumps are gone.
2. In a skillet over medium heat, melt butter and spread it around using a spatula.
3. Snip a small corner from the bag.
4. Working in batches, squeeze some of the batter into the hot skillet, cooking one or two cakes at a time.
5. Once corn cakes begin to bubble slightly, flip them onto their opposite sides. Cook briefly until golden brown.
6. Repeat steps 4 and 5 until all the batter is used.
7. Serve with honey.

Christine and Tim Conners
Tucson, Arizona

FINGER LAKES FRY BREAD

Total servings: 6 to 8
Preparation time: 1 hour
Challenge level: Moderate

V-LO

Preparation at camp:
1. Warm oil in skillet over medium-high heat.
2. Combine flour, salt, and baking powder in a bowl. Stir well.
3. Add water and honey to the bowl and stir into dough.
4. Knead the dough on a lightly floured surface until free of dry lumps, about 5 minutes.
5. Flatten dough into individual palm-size disks about ¼ inch thick.
6. Cooking in batches, fry dough disks in skillet for about 3 minutes on each side or until a light golden brown. Pause between batches with skillet off heat for a few minutes to allow oil to cool slightly.

Options:
Use as a bread to accompany a meal or dessert. Makes a great base for tacos, sloppy Joes, or folded sandwiches. Delicious sprinkled with garlic salt. Peanut butter and jelly create an open sandwich or even a dessert. Dusting with powdered sugar makes an open donut. Warmed canned pie filling on top is fantastic.

Ken Spiegel
Medford, New York

1 tablespoon vegetable oil

3 cups all-purpose flour

½ teaspoon salt

1 tablespoon baking powder

1½ cups water

2 tablespoons honey

Toppings: see options

Required equipment:
Medium-size skillet
Large mixing bowl

Snacks and Desserts

LUNA APPLES

Total servings: 2 to 4
Preparation time: 30 minutes
Challenge level: Easy

V

Looking for a simple, healthier dessert option to stare at the moon by? Try this delicious evening treat!

2 apples, cored and sliced into 8 pieces

¼ cup dried cranberries

4 teaspoons brown sugar

2 teaspoons ground cinnamon

¼ cup sliced almonds

Required equipment:
12-inch camp Dutch oven
Small mixing bowl
Pie pan

Preparation at camp:
1. Preheat Dutch oven using 17 coals on the lid and 8 coals under the oven.
2. Set sliced apples skin-side down in a pie pan.
3. Combine cranberries, sugar, cinnamon, and almonds in a small bowl. Mix well.
4. Pour cranberry and nut mix over the apples in the pie pan.
5. Set pan in oven, and with lid on, bake for about 10 minute or until apples are heated through.

Christine and Tim Conners
Tucson, Arizona

ELEVATION POPCORN

Total servings: 4
Preparation time: 30 minutes
Challenge level: Moderate

V-LO

Preparation at camp:
1. Coat bottom of Dutch oven with oil, then warm over 25 coals.
2. Evenly cover bottom of oven with popcorn kernels. Replace lid.
3. Cook the corn, rotating oven a quarter turn per minute to avoid hot spots.
4. Remove oven from coals once corn popping begins to slow. Don't wait too long on this step; otherwise, popcorn will burn!
5. Quickly and carefully pour popcorn into a large serving bowl.
6. Add softened butter to the warm popcorn, if desired, then salt or season to taste.

Tips:
When checking on the popcorn's progress, watch out for splattering oil! It takes practice to time popcorn just right. A little too short, and a lot of kernels remain. A little too long, and the corn burns. Be prepared for a couple of botched batches while you train your ear!

Christine and Tim Conners
Tucson, Arizona

¼ cup vegetable oil
¾ cup popcorn kernels
Softened butter and salt to taste
Optional toppings: garlic salt, furikake, Cajun seasoning, grated Parmesan cheese, butter powder, onion powder, powdered sugar

Required equipment:
12-inch camp Dutch oven
Large serving bowl

AUSTIN APPLES

Total servings: 4
Preparation time: 45 minutes
Challenge level: Easy

4 Granny Smith apples, skin on and cored

4 regular-size marshmallows

¼ cup cinnamon red hot candies

Required equipment:
8-inch camp Dutch oven
Heavy-duty aluminum foil

Preparation at camp:

1. Prepare 15 coals for the Dutch oven.
2. Stuff a marshmallow into the bottom section of each of the cored apples. The marshmallows serve as a plug to keep the candies from falling through.
3. Divide cinnamon candies among the 4 apples, filling the cores over the stuffed marshmallows.
4. Wrap each apple in foil.
5. Set wrapped apples upright in Dutch oven. Place lid on the oven.
6. Using 10 coals on the lid and 5 coals under the oven, bake for about 25 minutes, until apples are soft and steamy.

Tips:
To "core" an apple, carefully make a cylindrical cut around the core, then push it out. An apple corer is a kitchen utensil that can make the job easier.

Gerry Garges
Austin, Texas

COBSCOOK APPLE DUMPLINGS

Total servings: 4
Preparation time: 1 hour
Challenge level: Easy

V-LO

Preparation at camp:

1. Line Dutch oven with aluminum foil, pressing tightly into the perimeter around the bottom. Smooth the foil, eliminating bumps and bubbles.
2. Warm oven over 21 coals.
3. Melt the stick of butter in oven. Remove oven from the coals.
4. Add granulated and brown sugars to the oven and stir, being careful to avoid tearing the foil.
5. Wrap each slice of apple in one crescent roll, making 8 dumplings total. Add any optional ingredients to taste along with the apple.
6. Carefully and gently roll each wrapped apple in the hot melted sugar-butter. Lay each coated piece side-by-side in the oven.
7. Pour soda around the sides of the dumplings (not over the top of them!).
8. Move 14 coals to the lid, then set the oven over the remaining 7 coals. Bake for about 30 minutes, until the dumplings become a light golden brown.

Jim "Cinnamonboy" Rausch
Ellsworth, Maine

½ cup (1 standard stick) butter

⅓ cup granulated sugar

⅓ cup brown sugar

1 Granny Smith apple, cored, peeled, and sliced into 8 pieces

1 (8-ounce) package refrigerated crescent rolls

¾ cup Sprite or 7Up

Optional fillings to taste: ground cinnamon, ground ginger, ground cloves, apple pie spice, raisins, Craisins, walnuts

Required equipment:
10-inch camp Dutch oven
Aluminum foil

FANTASTIC FUDGE CAKE

V-LO

Total servings: 6 to 8
Preparation time: 1 hour
Challenge level: Easy

½ cup (1 standard stick) plus 3 tablespoons butter, softened

1 cup granulated sugar

2 eggs

2 teaspoons vanilla extract

⅓ cup plus 3 tablespoons unsweetened cocoa powder

½ cup self-rising flour

½ cup chopped walnuts

1 tablespoon honey

1 cup confectioners' sugar

1 tablespoon water

Required equipment:
10-inch camp Dutch oven
2 medium-size mixing bowls
Parchment paper

Preparation at camp:

1. Prepare 21 coals for the Dutch oven.
2. In a bowl, combine ½ cup butter, granulated sugar, eggs, 1 teaspoon vanilla extract, ⅓ cup cocoa powder, flour, and walnuts. Mix well.
3. Pour cake batter into a parchment-lined Dutch oven.
4. Bake using 14 coals on the lid and 7 coals under the oven for about 30 minutes.
5. While the cake is baking, prepare the topping by combining 3 tablespoons butter, 1 teaspoon vanilla extract, 3 tablespoons cocoa powder, honey, and confectioner's sugar. Gradually add the water while mixing to give it the consistency you prefer.
6. Pour topping over the cake once it is finished baking.

Option:
Chopped pecans can be substituted for the walnuts.

Christine and Tim Conners
Tucson, Arizona

SOPAPILLA CHEESECAKE

V-LO

Total servings: 6 to 8
Preparation time: 1 hour
Challenge level: Moderate

A decadent twist on a classic Mexican dessert.

Preparation at camp:

1. Prepare 25 coals for the Dutch oven.
2. Unroll and evenly spread dough from one container of crescent rolls over the bottom of a parchment-lined Dutch oven.
3. In a bowl, combine softened cream cheese, 1 cup sugar, and vanilla extract. Stir well.
4. Spread cream cheese mixture over crescent roll dough in oven.
5. Unroll and evenly spread dough from the remaining crescent roll container over the cream cheese mixture.
6. Melt butter in a small cook pot.
7. Pour melted butter over the top layer of crescent rolls.
8. In a cup, combine the remaining sugar and the ground cinnamon. Sprinkle over the crescent rolls.
9. Bake using 17 coals on the lid and 8 coals under the oven for 20 to 30 minutes or until crescent rolls become firm.

Jim Van Hecke
Albuquerque, New Mexico

2 (8-ounce) containers Pillsbury Butter Flake crescent rolls

2 (8-ounce) packages cream cheese, softened

1¼ cups granulated sugar

1 teaspoon vanilla extract

¼ cup (½ standard stick) butter

1 tablespoon ground cinnamon

Required equipment:
12-inch camp Dutch oven
Small cook pot
Medium-size mixing bowl
Parchment paper

CHILI CHOCOLATE CHIP ICE CREAM

Total servings: 6 to 8
Preparation time: 2 hours
Challenge level: Difficult

V-LO

I prepared this at a chili cook-off at the Merchant Marine Academy on Long Island. It took "Special Mention" because the judges said it wasn't real chili! The addition of the chili powder enhances the chocolate taste.

1½ cups whole milk

½ cup unsweetened cocoa powder

1 pint heavy whipping cream

1 teaspoon vanilla extract

1 cup milk chocolate chips

¼ teaspoon chili powder

Required equipment:
14-inch deep camp Dutch oven
10-inch camp Dutch oven
Small bag of ice
About 1 cup rock salt

Preparation at camp:

1. Spread an even layer of ice in the bottom of a 14-inch Dutch oven.
2. Sprinkle about ⅕ of the rock salt over the ice.
3. Set a 10-inch Dutch oven inside the 14-inch oven.
4. Pack the remaining space between the ovens with more ice and sprinkle with about ¼ of the remaining rock salt in the space between the ovens.
5. Allow ovens to chill for 15 minutes.
6. Meanwhile, mix milk, cocoa powder, heavy cream, and vanilla extract in a bowl until the cocoa fully dissolves.
7. Stir in the chocolate chips and chili powder.
8. Pour cream mixture into the 10-inch oven and cover with lid. If the 10-inch oven sits too high to allow the lid of the 14-inch oven to mostly close, invert cover of 10-inch oven. It's okay if the 14-inch won't fully close.
9. Completely pack the space around and on top of (not inside!) the 10-inch oven with more ice. Evenly pour about ½ of the remaining rock salt over the ice. Set lid on 14-inch oven.
10. Every 30 minutes or so, remove the ice from the lid of the smaller oven and scrape the ice cream from the wall of the oven. Avoid getting ice and rock salt into the ice cream when doing this! Scraping the cream from the wall helps the ice cream to freeze more uniformly.

11. Replace lid on 10-inch oven and add more ice and rock salt as necessary.
12. Check back every 30 minutes to scrape ice cream from the oven wall.
13. Serve once ice cream has thickened to your liking. Expect this to take about 60 to 90 minutes after first setting the lid over the cream mixture.

Tips:
An 8-inch camp Dutch oven will also work for the smaller oven in this recipe. If you don't have a smaller oven, a metal bowl with a sealable cover can be substituted.

Ken Spiegel
Medford, New York

GRUMPY'S DUMP CAKE

Total servings: 8
Preparation time: 1 hour
Challenge level: Easy

V-LO

1 (15.25-ounce) package chocolate cake mix

1 (3.9-ounce) package chocolate fudge instant pudding mix

1½ cups whole milk

1 (10.5-ounce) package Reese's Miniature Cups

Required equipment:
10-inch camp Dutch oven
Large mixing bowl
Parchment paper

Preparation at camp:

1. Prepare 21 coals for the Dutch oven.

2. In a bowl, combine the cake and pudding mixes with the milk. Stir well to break up clumps.

3. Remove wrappers from the Reese's cups, then chop the cups into bits. Fold pieces into the batter.

4. Line Dutch oven with parchment paper.

5. Pour cake batter into the oven.

6. Bake using 14 coals on the lid and 7 coals under the oven for about 35 minutes or until an inserted knife comes out clean. Serve warm.

Options:
Serve with whipped cream or vanilla ice cream!

Michael "Grumpy" Wyatt
Noblesville, Indiana

APPLE BETTY

V-LO

Total servings: 8
Preparation time: 1 hour
Challenge level: Easy

Preparation at camp:
1. Prepare 21 coals for the Dutch oven.
2. In a bowl, combine apples, graham cracker crumbs, sugar, cinnamon, and nutmeg.
3. Pour apple mixture into a parchment-lined Dutch oven.
4. Lay butter slices evenly over apple mixture.
5. Pour apple cider over mixture.
6. Bake using 14 coals on top and 7 coals under the oven for about 30 minutes.
7. Cut into wedges and serve warm with whipped cream.

Tip:
Graham cracker crumbs can be found prepackaged at the grocery store.

Ken Vetrovec
Racine, Wisconsin

3 large green apples, cored, peeled, and chopped

1½ cups graham cracker crumbs

1 cup brown sugar

1 teaspoon ground cinnamon

1 teaspoon ground nutmeg

¼ cup (½ standard stick) butter, cut into slices

½ cup apple cider

1 can whipped cream

Required equipment:
10-inch camp Dutch oven
Large mixing bowl
Parchment paper

GORILLA BREAD

Total servings: 8
Preparation time: 1 hour
Challenge level: Moderate

V-LO

1 tablespoon ground cinnamon

¼ cup granulated sugar

½ cup (1 standard stick) butter, softened

1 cup brown sugar

1 cup chopped pecans

1 (16.3-ounce) container refrigerated biscuit dough

1 (8-ounce) package cream cheese, cut into 8 pieces

Required equipment:
10-inch camp Dutch oven
Small mixing bowl
Parchment paper

Preparation at camp:

1. Prepare 21 coals for the Dutch oven.
2. Combine cinnamon and granulated sugar in a bowl.
3. In a parchment-lined Dutch oven, spread butter over parchment then evenly cover with brown sugar and nuts.
4. On a smooth, clean surface, flatten each of the refrigerated biscuits, 8 total.
5. Sprinkle about half of the cinnamon-sugar mixture over the top of all the biscuits.
6. Set one piece of cream cheese on each biscuit, then roll up the dough to seal.
7. Place rolled-up biscuits, seam-side down, over the sugar-nut mixture in the oven.
8. Sprinkle biscuits with the remaining cinnamon-sugar mixture.
9. Bake using 14 coals on the lid and 7 coals under the oven for about 30 minutes or until the tops are a light golden brown.

Option:
Try substituting walnuts for the pecans.

Carl Laub
Arlington Heights, Illinois

COCONUT PECAN PIE

V-LO

Total servings: 8
Preparation time: 1 hour 15 minutes
Challenge level: Easy

Incredibly delicious!

Preparation at camp:
1. Preheat Dutch oven using 17 coals on the lid and 8 coals under the oven.
2. In a large mixing bowl, combine the sugars, eggs, softened butter, buttermilk, coconut, pecans, flour, and vanilla extract. Mix well.
3. Pour pie filling into the prebaked piecrust.
4. Place pie on a trivet in the oven and bake for about 55 minutes, until the pie is golden brown and the center is barely set.

Option:
If you can't find a prebaked piecrust, simply bake a premade crust in its foil pan for a few minutes in the heated Dutch oven before adding the filling.

Tip:
A trivet is a small platform used to elevate a baking pan from a heated surface to provide more even heating and to prevent scorching. At camp, a makeshift trivet can easily be made by using three small stones to support the pan in the oven.

Robert "Cowboy Bob" Dowdy
Great Falls, Montana

1⅓ cups granulated sugar

1 pinch brown sugar

3 eggs

¼ cup (½ standard stick) butter, softened

½ cup buttermilk

1½ cups sweetened flaked coconut

3 ounces chopped pecans

1 tablespoon all-purpose flour

1 teaspoon vanilla extract

1 9-inch prebaked piecrust

Required equipment:
12-inch camp Dutch oven
Large mixing bowl
Trivet

AWARD-WINNING APPLE-CRANBERRY COBBLER

Total servings: 8 to 10
Preparation time: 1 hour
Challenge level: Easy

V-LO

I prepared a version of this recipe a number of years ago for a Scoutmasters' cooking competition and won!

1 (21-ounce) can apple pie filling

1 (14-ounce) can whole-berry cranberry sauce

2 cups chopped walnuts

1 (12.4-ounce) container Pillsbury refrigerated cinnamon rolls with icing

Required equipment:
10-inch camp Dutch oven

Preparation at camp:

1. Prepare 23 coals for the Dutch oven.
2. Combine apple pie filling and cranberry sauce in Dutch oven and stir.
3. Evenly spread 1 cup chopped walnuts over apple-cranberry mixture.
4. Separate cinnamon roll dough into individual pieces, then slice each roll into two disks.
5. Distribute disks evenly over nuts and fruit filling.
6. Evenly sprinkle the remaining walnuts over the rolls.
7. Using 16 coals on the lid and 7 coals under the oven, bake for 30 to 40 minutes, until rolls are a light golden brown.
8. Drizzle icing from dough container over rolls and serve.

Mike Russell
Harker Heights, Texas

CARAMEL APPLE PIE COBBLER

Total servings: 8 to 10
Preparation time: 1 hour
Challenge level: Easy

V-LO

Preparation at camp:

1. Prepare 21 coals for the Dutch oven.
2. Cover bottom of a parchment-lined Dutch oven with apple pie filling.
3. In a medium-size bowl, combine Bisquick and water. Mix well.
4. Cover apple pie filling with Bisquick batter, then bake using 14 coals on the lid and 7 coals under the oven for about 20 minutes.
5. Meanwhile, in a small bowl, combine cinnamon, brown sugar, and oats. Stir well.
6. Once batter has cooked for 20 minutes, remove oven from heat and evenly distribute butter slices over the top.
7. Sprinkle the oat mix over all, then decorate with caramel topping to taste.
8. Cover with lid and place back over coals. Continue cooking for an additional 15 minutes, until the cobbler is heated through.

John Krauss, Jr.
Kirtland, Ohio

1 (21-ounce) can apple pie filling

1 cup Bisquick Heart Smart pancake and baking mix

¾ cup water

1 teaspoon ground cinnamon

½ cup brown sugar

½ cup quick oats

½ cup (1 standard stick) butter, cut into slices

Caramel topping to taste

Required equipment:
10-inch camp Dutch oven
Small mixing bowl
Medium-size mixing bowl
Parchment paper

MISTER LARRY'S COBBLER

V-LO

Total servings: 8 to 10
Preparation time: 1 hour 15 minutes
Challenge level: Moderate

This recipe comes from Mr. Larry Andrews of Dothan, Alabama. I've tried many cobblers, and this is one of the best!

½ cup (1 standard stick) butter

2 cups Bisquick pancake mix

1 cup water

½ cup granulated sugar

1 (21-ounce) can blueberry pie filling

1 (5-ounce) can evaporated milk

Toppings: vanilla ice cream or whipped cream

Required equipment:
10-inch camp Dutch oven
Medium-size mixing bowl
Parchment paper

Preparation at camp:

1. Prepare 23 coals the Dutch oven.

2. Line the inside of Dutch oven with parchment paper.

3. Cut the stick of butter into thin slices and evenly distribute half of the slices over the parchment paper on the bottom of the oven.

4. Mix Bisquick and water in a bowl to form a spreadable dough.

5. Spread dough evenly over butter on the bottom of the oven.

6. Add the next three ingredients in layers: the sugar, then the pie filling, and ending with the evaporated milk. Do not stir!

7. Distribute the remaining butter slices across the top of the cobbler.

8. Bake for about 45 minutes using 16 coals on the lid and 7 coals under the oven.

9. Top with vanilla ice cream or whipped cream.

Option:
Substitute your favorite pie filling for the blueberry.

Debbie Fowler
Dothan, Alabama

PINEAPPLE CASSEROLE

Total servings: 10 to 12
Preparation time: 1 hour
Challenge level: Easy

V-LO

Preparation at camp:
1. Prepare 21 coals for the Dutch oven.
2. Mix pineapple, sugar, flour, and cheese in a bowl.
3. In a parchment-lined Dutch oven, evenly spread two sleeves of crushed crackers over the bottom of the oven.
4. Evenly cover crackers with the pineapple mixture.
5. Top with the crushed crackers from the two remaining sleeves.
6. Lay butter slices over the top of the crackers.
7. Bake using 14 coals on the lid and 7 coals under the oven for about 40 minutes, until mixture is heated through and the top is a light brown.

Christine and Tim Conners
Tucson, Arizona

1 (20-ounce) can pineapple tidbits with juice
1 cup granulated sugar
1 cup all-purpose flour
2 cups shredded cheddar cheese
1 (13.7-ounce) package Ritz crackers, crushed
½ cup (1 standard stick) butter, cut into slices

Required equipment:
10-inch camp Dutch oven
Large mixing bowl
Parchment paper

DUTCH OVEN ICE CREAM

Total servings: 8 to 10
Preparation time: 2 hours
Challenge level: Difficult

V-LO

This is a basic recipe that can be easily altered to create a variety of fun ice cream combos! Make sure your oven is thoroughly cleaned so flavors from previous use don't transfer to the ice cream.

1 quart half-and-half

1 (14-ounce) can sweetened condensed milk

Optional ingredients: vanilla extract, chocolate chips, cocoa powder, chopped nuts, shredded coconut, Heath English Toffee Bits, chopped fresh fruit, gummy bears

Optional toppings: fudge, caramel, butterscotch, pineapple, strawberry

Required equipment:
10-inch camp Dutch oven
Large tub or cooler
Large mixing bowl
Large bag of ice
1 cup rock salt

Preparation at camp:

1. Combine half-and-half and sweetened condensed milk in a large bowl. If you'd like vanilla flavor, now is the time to add 1 tablespoon vanilla extract. Mix well.

2. Add about 2 inches of crushed ice to the bottom of a large clean tub or cooler with the capacity to hold a 10-inch Dutch oven.

3. Sprinkle about half of the rock salt over the ice. Set Dutch oven on top of the ice.

4. Pack gap between oven and sides of tub with more crushed ice and the remainder of the rock salt. Keep the level of the ice and salt at least 1 to 2 inches below the rim of the Dutch oven to keep salt water from accidentally sloshing into the ice cream.

5. Carefully pour water over the ice around the sides of the Dutch oven to create a 2-inch-deep slurry at the bottom of the tub. The water should reach the underside of the oven. Allow oven to chill for about 10 minutes.

6. Pour ice cream mixture into the cold 10-inch Dutch oven.

7. Place lid on oven, and cover lid completely with crushed ice. Do not put rock salt on the lid.

8. About 30 minutes after adding the lid to the oven, begin stirring the ice cream every 10 minutes, scraping the mixture from the walls of the oven using a spatula.

9. When the ice cream begins to firm and becomes difficult to stir, add your optional ingredients and mix carefully. Freezing time will depend on a number of factors, but expect it to start firming about 60 to 90 minutes after first setting the lid on the oven.
10. Serve with optional toppings.

Jim "Cinnamonboy" Rausch
Ellsworth, Maine

CARRIBBEAN PINEAPPLE UPSIDE-DOWN CAKE

Total servings: 10 to 12
Preparation time: 1 hour 15 minutes
Challenge level: Difficult

V-LO

1 (20-ounce) can sliced pineapple rings, juice reserved

1 (15.25-ounce) package Duncan Hines yellow cake mix

½ cup vegetable oil

3 eggs

½ cup (1 standard stick) butter, softened

1½ cups brown sugar

⅓ cup rum

6 maraschino cherries

Required equipment:
10-inch camp Dutch oven
Large mixing bowl
Large serving plate
Heavy-duty cooking mitts
Heavy-duty aluminum foil

Preparation at camp:

1. Prepare 21 coals for the Dutch oven.
2. Drain juice from the pineapple can into a bowl. Add cake mix, oil, and eggs to the bowl and mix well.
3. Line Dutch oven with foil, pressing the foil into the perimeter around the bottom of oven.
4. Set 7 coals under the oven. Combine butter, brown sugar, and rum in the oven and heat until it bubbles. Stir carefully to avoid tearing foil.
5. Evenly distribute 6 pineapple rings over the mixture. Place a cherry at the center of each of the rings.
6. Chop remaining pineapple rings into small pieces and add to batter. Pour batter into oven.
7. Place 14 coals on the lid, keeping the 7 coals underneath. Bake for 35 to 40 minutes or until a knife inserted into the batter comes out clean. Refresh coals as needed.
8. Using heavy-duty cooking mitts, place a large plate over the top of the open oven, then carefully flip the oven and plate upside down together to drop the cake onto the plate.
9. Remove foil from the cake and serve.

Tip:
This is an easy recipe up until the oven needs to be flipped. Request assistance for this step if you're not sure you can handle it by yourself!

Christine and Tim Conners
Tucson, Arizona

GREAT FALLS CARAMEL PECAN BREAD PUDDING

V-LO

Total servings: 10 to 12
Preparation time: 1 hour 30 minutes
Challenge level: Easy

Preparation at camp:

1. Prepare 21 coals for the Dutch oven.
2. Line Dutch oven with parchment paper and spread ½ cup (1 standard stick) softened butter over the paper at bottom of oven.
3. Combine flour, 1 cup sugar, and milk in a bowl. Mix well and pour over the butter in the oven. Spread the batter evenly.
4. In a second bowl, combine ½ cup (1 standard stick) softened butter, eggs, ⅔ cup sugar, Karo syrup, and pecans. Pour filling evenly over batter.
5. Bake using 14 coals on the lid and 7 coals under the oven for about 1 hour or until the batter becomes firm.

Robert "Cowboy Bob" Dowdy
Great Falls, Montana

1 cup (2 standard sticks) butter, softened

1 cup self-rising flour

1⅔ cups granulated sugar

1 cup whole milk

4 eggs, beaten

1½ cups dark Karo corn syrup

2 cups chopped pecans

½ teaspoon vanilla extract

Required equipment:
10-inch camp Dutch oven
2 medium-size mixing bowls
Parchment paper

BRECKENRIDGE MOUNTAIN BROWNIES

V-LO

Total servings: 10 to 12
Preparation time: 1 hour 30 minutes
Challenge level: Moderate

1⅔ cups granulated sugar

1¼ cups (2½ standard sticks) butter, softened

2 tablespoons water

2 large eggs

1 tablespoon vanilla extract

1⅓ cups all-purpose flour

¾ cup plus ⅔ cup cocoa powder

½ teaspoon baking powder

¼ teaspoon salt

1 cup chopped nuts (your favorite)

3 cups confectioners' sugar

⅓ cup whole milk

Required equipment:
10-inch camp Dutch oven
2 medium-size mixing bowls
Parchment paper

Preparation at camp:

1. Prepare 21 coals for the Dutch oven.

2. In a bowl, prepare batter by combining granulated sugar, ¾ cup butter, water, eggs, and 2 teaspoons vanilla extract. Stir well.

3. In a second bowl, mix flour, ¾ cup cocoa powder, baking powder, and salt.

4. Blend flour-cocoa mixture into batter. Add nuts and stir.

5. Spread brownie batter into a parchment-lined Dutch oven.

6. Bake for 30 to 40 minutes using 14 coals on the lid and 7 coals under the oven. Brownies will be ready once an inserted knife comes out clean.

7. While the brownies bake, and reusing the bowl used to prepare the flour-cocoa mixture, prepare the frosting by combining confectioner's sugar, ⅔ cup cocoa powder, ½ cup butter, milk, and 1 teaspoon vanilla extract. Stir until creamy.

8. Allow brownies to cool, uncovered, for about 20 to 30 minutes.

9. Spread frosting over brownies and serve.

Christine and Tim Conners
Tucson, Arizona

194

WILD BERRY POUND CAKE

V-LO

Total servings: 10 to 12
Preparation time: 1 hour 45 minutes
Challenge level: Easy

Preparation at camp:

1. Prepare 23 coals for the Dutch oven.
2. Line Dutch oven with parchment paper, then grease paper with 1 tablespoon of butter.
3. Sprinkle ¼ cup sugar over the butter in the oven.
4. Cream the remaining 1 cup of softened butter with the remaining 2 cups of sugar, the eggs, and the vanilla extract. Mix thoroughly.
5. In a separate bowl, combine flour, salt, and baking powder.
6. Add flour mix to the creamed mixture and stir well to combine.
7. Carefully fold blueberries into the batter.
8. Scoop batter evenly into bottom of the oven.
9. Place 16 coals on the lid and 7 coals under the oven. Bake for about 1 hour and 10 minutes, or until the center of the pound cake is firm.
10. Allow pound cake to cool for about 10 minutes before serving.

Emily Kochetta
Statesboro, Georgia

1 cup plus 1 tablespoon butter, softened

2¼ cups granulated sugar

4 eggs

1 teaspoon vanilla extract

2¾ cups all-purpose flour

½ teaspoon salt

1 teaspoon baking powder

3 cups fresh blueberries

Required equipment:
12-inch camp Dutch oven
2 medium-size mixing bowls
Parchment paper

GLAMPER'S CHOCOLATE CHIP DREAM CAKE

V-LO

Total servings: 12 to 14
Preparation time: 1 hour
Challenge level: Moderate

Yes, there are campers who have actually survived a weekend or two without chocolate. But let's be honest: the quality of the experience must have been tarnished. Fortunately, there's no need for you to suffer: Andrea Kippes has made it easy to experience the euphoria of a rich, chocolaty treat!

Cake:
1 (15.25-ounce) package devil's food cake mix

1 (3.9-ounce) package instant chocolate pudding mix

1 cup sour cream

4 large eggs

½ cup water

½ cup vegetable oil

1½ cups mini chocolate chips

Frosting:
1 (8-ounce) package cream cheese, softened

¼ cup (½ standard stick) butter, softened

1 teaspoon vanilla extract

2½ cups powdered sugar

Required equipment:
12-inch camp Dutch oven
Large mixing bowl
Medium-size bowl
Parchment paper
Quart-size ziplock bag

Preparation at camp:
1. Prepare 25 coals for the Dutch oven.
2. While coals are heating, combine cake mix, instant pudding mix, sour cream, eggs, water, and oil in a large bowl.
3. Mix ingredients well, then stir in chocolate chips, reserving some, if desired, for topping.
4. Pour cake batter into a parchment-lined Dutch oven. Cover with lid.
5. Set 17 coals on the lid and 8 coals underneath the oven.
6. Bake, rotating lid and oven a quarter turn in opposite directions every 10 to 15 minutes.
7. At 35 minutes, check doneness by touching cake surface. Once ready, cake will bounce back gently. A skewer or knife inserted should come out clean, with no batter adhering.
8. Meanwhile, prepare frosting by beating cream cheese and butter together in a medium-size bowl until fully mixed and fluffy.
9. Add vanilla extract to cream cheese blend. Gradually stir in powdered sugar until thick.
10. Transfer frosting to a quart-size ziplock bag. Once cake is ready, snip a corner from the bag and squeeze frosting over cake in a pattern. Sprinkle with any reserved chocolate chips.

Andrea Kippes
San Jose, California

196

WAIMEA BAY MANGO COBBLER

Total servings: 12 to 14
Preparation time: 1 hour 30 minutes
Challenge level: Moderate

V-LO

Our Scout troop created this recipe while at Camp Pupukea in Hawaii. The director had a mango tree in his yard and brought the fruit to camp. We combined the fresh mango with ingredients found at the dining hall for the cobbler cook-off competition. The recipe was a major hit!

Preparation at camp:

1. Prepare 25 coals for the Dutch oven.
2. Remove skin from mangos, then cut each into bite-size pieces while removing the large, thin seed.
3. Mix all filling ingredients, including mango, in a large bowl.
4. Line oven with aluminum foil, then grease the foil with cooking spray or oil.
5. Pour mango filling into the Dutch oven, spreading it evenly.
6. Mix all topping ingredients, except cinnamon, in a medium-size bowl.
7. Pour topping mixture over mango filling. Spread topping evenly, but do not stir it into the filling! It's supposed to lay on top.
8. Sprinkle ground cinnamon over the topping.
9. Bake for about 60 minutes using 17 coals on the lid of the Dutch oven and 8 coals underneath. Refresh coals as required.

Tim Moberly
South Elgin, Illinois

Filling:
10 ripe mangos
½ cup granulated sugar
½ cup all-purpose flour
1 tablespoon lemon juice
1 teaspoon ground cinnamon

Topping:
1½ cups brown sugar
1½ cups all-purpose flour
1½ cups old-fashioned oats
½ cup (1 standard stick) butter, softened
½ teaspoon ground cinnamon

Required equipment:
12-inch camp Dutch oven
Large mixing bowl
Medium-size mixing bowl
Cooking spray or vegetable oil
Heavy-duty aluminum foil

CHEESECAKE WITH CARAMEL APPLE STREUSEL TOPPING

Total servings: 12 to 14
Preparation time: 1 hour 30 minutes
Challenge level: Difficult

V-LO

If there are any doubters questioning why the Dutch oven remains such a popular outdoor cooking device after all these years, perhaps it's because they've never tried this recipe!

Crust:
1½ cups all-purpose flour

⅓ cup brown sugar

¾ cup (1½ standard sticks) butter, softened

Cheesecake filling:
2 (8-ounce) packages cream cheese, softened

½ cup granulated sugar

1 teaspoon vanilla extract

2 large eggs

Apple topping:
2 large Granny Smith apples, cored, peeled, and finely chopped

2 tablespoons granulated sugar

¼ teaspoon ground nutmeg

½ teaspoon ground cinnamon

Streusel topping:
1 cup brown sugar

1 cup all-purpose flour

½ cup quick oats

½ cup (1 standard stick) butter, softened

Preparation at camp:
1. Prepare 25 coals for the Dutch oven.
2. To prepare crust mixture, combine flour and brown sugar in a medium-size bowl. Cut in butter until crumbly.
3. Press crust mixture evenly into bottom of a parchment-lined Dutch oven. Bake for about 15 minutes using 17 coals on lid and 8 coals underneath the oven.
4. While crust is baking, prepare cheesecake filling by beating cream cheese in a large bowl along with granulated sugar until smooth. Add vanilla extract and eggs to bowl. Mix well but do not over-beat.
5. Remove oven from coals and evenly pour filling over crust in oven.
6. In a second medium-size bowl, prepare apple topping by stirring together chopped apples, granulated sugar, nutmeg, and cinnamon.
7. Spoon apple topping evenly over cream cheese mixture in oven.
8. Wipe the bowl used for the apple topping, and use the bowl to prepare streusel topping by combining brown sugar, flour, and oats. Cut butter into topping mixture.
9. Evenly sprinkle streusel topping over apples in oven.
10. Return lid to oven and continue baking for 30 minutes or until filling is set. Refresh coals as required.
11. While cheesecake is baking, prepare the caramel topping by combining cream, evaporated milk, brown sugar, butter, and salt in a small pot heated over a camp stove

or a few hot coals. Stir frequently, bringing caramel topping to a boil until thick, about 10 to 15 minutes.

12. Remove caramel topping from heat, then stir in vanilla extract.

13. Once cheesecake is ready, drizzle caramel topping over the top and serve.

Lisa Blodgett
West Jordan, Utah

Caramel topping:

½ cup heavy cream

½ cup evaporated milk

½ cup brown sugar

1 tablespoon butter

1 pinch salt

½ teaspoon vanilla extract

Required equipment:

12-inch camp Dutch oven
Small cook pot
2 medium-size mixing bowls
Large mixing bowl
Parchment paper

BACKYARD BAKLAVA

Total servings: 14 to 16
Preparation time: 1 hour 45 minutes (plus 1 to 2 hours to cool)
Challenge level: Difficult

V-LO

Looking for a challenge with a huge, sweet reward at the end? Look no further.

1 teaspoon vegetable oil

3 cups chopped walnuts

2 teaspoons ground cinnamon

3 cups granulated sugar

2 cups water

½ cup honey

1 lemon, juiced

1 pound butter

1 pound phyllo dough, thawed

Preparation at camp:

1. In a skillet, warm oil over medium heat and toast the nuts.
2. In a bowl, toss toasted nuts with the cinnamon and set aside.
3. In a cook pot over medium heat, combine sugar, water, honey, and lemon juice and bring to a low boil for about 10 minutes. Cool.
4. Wipe the skillet, then use it to melt the butter. Remove skillet from heat.
5. Prepare 21 coals for the Dutch oven.
6. Line Dutch oven with parchment paper.
7. Carefully dip a folded paper towel in the melted butter and use it to grease the parchment in the bottom of the oven.
8. Tear a sheet of phyllo to fit the Dutch oven, then brush it with butter. Place a second sheet and brush it with butter also. Repeat the process until about ¼ of the phyllo sheets are used.
9. Evenly cover phyllo in the oven with a layer of about ⅓ of the nut filling.
10. Repeat steps 8 and 9 twice more. There should be no more nut filling remaining, but some of the phyllo sheets should remain.
11. Cover all with the remaining phyllo, brushing it with the remaining butter. Tuck in the edges along the wall of the oven.
12. Slice a diamond-shaped repetitive pattern into the top layers of dough, but don't cut all the way through.
13. Bake using 14 coals on the lid and 7 under the oven for 1 hour. Refresh coals as needed.

14. Pour cooled syrup over hot baklava. The syrup should mostly cover the top layer.
15. Allow baklava to cool for an hour or two, lid removed, with a towel draped over the top of oven.
16. Be sure to cut all the way through the bottom layer when serving.

Options:
Try almonds, pecans, or hazelnuts instead of the walnuts, or a combination of all of them!

Tip:
Phyllo dough can be found in the freezer section of large grocery stores.

Mike "Mountain Man Mike" Lancaster
Clovis, California

Required equipment:
10-inch camp Dutch oven
Medium-size skillet
Medium-size cook pot
Medium-size bowl
Parchment paper

ENGLISH CHEESECAKE

Total servings: 12 to 14
Preparation time: 2 hours
Challenge level: Difficult

V-LO

This is classic cheesecake with an English twist! I was participating in a Dutch oven competition at the time of the 2012 Olympics, held in London that year. I thought the shortbread crust would fit nicely with the theme!

Crust:
5 tablespoons butter

2 cups crushed shortbread cookies

2 tablespoons granulated sugar

Batter:
5 (8-ounce) packages cream cheese, softened

1 cup granulated sugar

3 tablespoons all-purpose flour

1 tablespoon vanilla extract

1 cup sour cream

4 eggs

1 cup toffee chips

Required equipment:
12-inch camp Dutch oven
Small cook pot
Large mixing bowl
Parchment paper

Preparation at camp:

1. Prepare 23 coals for the Dutch oven.
2. Melt butter in a pot over low heat.
3. Mix together crushed cookies, sugar, and melted butter in a bowl.
4. Line Dutch oven with parchment paper and evenly press the cookie mixture into the bottom and perimeter of the oven.
5. Bake crust for 5 to 7 minutes using 16 coals on the lid and 7 coals under the oven.
6. While crust is baking, wipe the bowl clean.
7. Remove oven from coals and allow oven to cool.
8. In the cleaned bowl, combine cream cheese, sugar, flour, and vanilla extract. Mix well.
9. Blend in sour cream, then add one egg at a time until fully mixed.
10. Pour batter over now-cooled crust.
11. Cover oven and bake using 16 coals on the lid and 7 coals under the oven for 1 hour or until center of cheesecake has set. Refresh coals as needed.
12. Remove oven from coals and sprinkle toffee chips over top.
13. Cover oven for a few additional minutes, allowing chips to melt.
14. Remove from heat and allow to cool before serving.

Chris Bryant
Pottstown, Pennsylvania

PIE IRON FRUIT PIE

Total servings: 1
Preparation time: 20 minutes
Challenge level: Moderate

V-LO

Preparation at camp:
1. Coat inside of the pie iron with butter.
2. Cut out two rectangular pieces of pie dough large enough to fit inside pie iron.
3. Position one of the pieces of pie dough in one side of the pie iron.
4. Top the dough in pie iron with pie filling, centering it toward the middle of the dough and away from the edges.
5. Lay second dough piece over the ingredients in the pie iron and tightly seal the edges of the first and second pieces of dough.
6. Close the iron and cook for about 5 minutes on each side over the heat of a campfire or grill. Do not hold the pie iron directly in the flame for an extended length of time or dough may burn.
7. Remove iron from heat, open the iron, and very carefully remove the contents.

Tip:
This recipe is appropriate for a pie iron roughly 4 by 4 inches square. For a pie iron of different size, scale the ingredients accordingly, remembering that precision isn't critical here.

Christine and Tim Conners
Tucson, Arizona

1 teaspoon butter, softened

1 premade refrigerated pie dough

3 tablespoons blueberry, strawberry, or apple pie filling

Required equipment:
Pie iron

PIE IRON PEANUT BUTTER AND BANANA DELIGHT

Total servings: 1
Preparation time: 20 minutes
Challenge level: Moderate

V-LO

1 teaspoon butter, softened

2 slices bread

2 tablespoons peanut butter

⅓ banana, thinly sliced

Optional: chopped nuts and milk chocolate chips

Required equipment:
Pie iron

Preparation at camp:

1. Coat inside of the pie iron with butter.
2. Trim bread to fit inside pie iron, then place a slice in each side of the iron.
3. Spread 1 tablespoon peanut butter on each slice of the bread.
4. Distribute banana slices over the peanut butter. Add optional nuts and chocolate chips at this time.
5. Seal iron and cook for about 5 minutes on each side over the heat of a campfire or grill. Do not hold the pie iron directly in the flame for an extended length of time or bread may burn.
6. Remove iron from heat, open the iron, and very carefully remove contents.

Tip:
This recipe is appropriate for a pie iron roughly 4 by 4 inches square. For a pie iron of different size, scale the ingredients accordingly, remembering that precision isn't critical here.

Ken Spiegel
Medford, New York

APPENDIX A: COMMON MEASUREMENT CONVERSIONS

US Volumetric Conversions

1 smidgen	$\frac{1}{32}$ teaspoon
1 pinch	$\frac{1}{16}$ teaspoon
1 dash	$\frac{1}{8}$ teaspoon
3 teaspoons	1 tablespoon
48 teaspoons	1 cup
2 tablespoons	$\frac{1}{8}$ cup
4 tablespoons	$\frac{1}{4}$ cup
5 tablespoons + 1 teaspoon	$\frac{1}{3}$ cup
8 tablespoons	$\frac{1}{2}$ cup
12 tablespoons	$\frac{3}{4}$ cup
16 tablespoons	1 cup
1 ounce	2 tablespoons
4 ounces	$\frac{1}{2}$ cup
8 ounces	1 cup
$\frac{5}{8}$ cup	$\frac{1}{2}$ cup + 2 tablespoons
$\frac{7}{8}$ cup	$\frac{3}{4}$ cup + 2 tablespoons
2 cups	1 pint
2 pints	1 quart
1 quart	4 cups
4 quarts	1 gallon
1 gallon	128 ounces

Note: Dry and fluid volumes are equivalent for teaspoon, tablespoon, and cup.

International Metric System Conversions

Volume and Weight

United States	*Metric*
¼ teaspoon	1.25 milliliters
½ teaspoon	2.50 milliliters
¾ teaspoon	3.75 milliliters
1 teaspoon	5 milliliters
1 tablespoon	15 milliliters
1 ounce (volume)	30 milliliters
¼ cup	60 milliliters
½ cup	120 milliliters
¾ cup	180 milliliters
1 cup	240 milliliters
1 pint	0.48 liter
1 quart	0.95 liter
1 gallon	3.79 liters
1 ounce (weight)	28 grams
1 pound	0.45 kilogram

Temperature

°F	*°C*
175	80
200	95
225	105
250	120
275	135
300	150
325	165
350	175
375	190
400	205
425	220
450	230
475	245
500	260

British, Canadian, and Australian Conversions

1 teaspoon (Britain, Canada, Australia)	approx. 1 teaspoon (United States)
1 tablespoon (Britain, Canada)	approx. 1 tablespoon (United States)
1 tablespoon (Australia)	1.35 tablespoons (United States)
1 ounce (Britain, Canada, Australia)	0.96 ounce (United States)
1 gill (Britain)	5 ounces (Britain, Canada, Australia)
1 cup (Britain)	10 ounces (Britain, Canada, Australia)
1 cup (Britain)	9.61 ounces (United States)
1 cup (Britain)	1.20 cups (United States)
1 cup (Canada, Australia)	8.45 ounces (United States)
1 cup (Canada, Australia)	1.06 cups (United States)
1 pint (Britain, Canada, Australia)	20 ounces (Britain, Canada, Australia)
1 imperial gallon (Britain)	1.20 gallons (United States)
1 pound (Britain, Canada, Australia)	1 pound (United States)

Equivalent Measures*

16 ounces water	1 pound
2 cups vegetable oil	1 pound
2 cups, or 4 sticks, butter	1 pound
2 cups granulated sugar	1 pound
3½ to 4 cups unsifted confectioners' sugar	1 pound
2¼ cups packed brown sugar	1 pound
4 cups sifted flour	1 pound
3½ cups unsifted whole wheat flour	1 pound
8–10 egg whites	1 cup
12–14 egg yolks	1 cup
1 whole lemon, squeezed	3 tablespoons juice
1 whole orange, squeezed	⅓ cup juice

* Approximate

APPENDIX B: SOURCES OF EQUIPMENT AND SUPPLIES

Amazon

www.amazon.com

It's well-known that Amazon sells an enormous array of products. But it might come as a surprise that it also hosts a very large number of vendors who sell exotic food ingredients difficult to find in your local grocery store. Check out Amazon if you're stumped when trying to locate an ingredient.

Bass Pro Shops

www.basspro.com

Bass Pro stocks a large line of kitchen gear perfect for camping, including a wide array of Lodge Dutch ovens and accessories. Bass Pro stores are a good place to go to see the equipment firsthand before you buy.

Bulk Foods

www.bulkfoods.com

Here you'll find an enormous selection of dried fruits, spices, grains, and nuts sold in a variety of sizes and quantities.

Camp Chef

www.campchef.com

Many camp cooking accessories are available through Camp Chef. The company also markets its own line of cast iron Dutch ovens, frying pans, and other cookware.

Campmor

www.campmor.com

Campmor stocks a huge selection of general camping supplies, many of them valuable for rounding out a list of basic equipment for a remotely located camp kitchen, farther from your vehicle.

Chuck Wagon Supply

www.chuckwagonsupply.com

The range of cast iron cookware and accessories at Chuck Wagon is impressive. This is a great site to compare different Dutch oven makes and models and to discover all those items you didn't know you needed. The company posts a wealth of helpful information for those new to cast iron cooking.

Costco

www.costco.com

This popular membership warehouse stocks serving ware in package sizes perfect for large groups. Retail stores are located throughout North America.

Dutch Oven Gear

www.dutchovengear.com

Sami Dahdal is CEO of Sam's Iron Works and its sister company, Dutch Oven Gear. A master wrought-iron craftsman, Sam manufactures quality tables and accessories for camp Dutch ovens. Check the website to see his gear in action.

Lodge Manufacturing

www.lodgemfg.com

Founded in 1896, Lodge is the premier source of a large array of high-quality cast iron cookware and related accessories.

REI

www.rei.com

Like Campmor, REI carries a wide array of gear useful for the camp kitchen. REI also stocks an assortment of cast iron cookware and accessories by Lodge.

Sam's Club

www.samsclub.com

Sam's Club, like Costco, is a large membership warehouse. Sam's has hundreds of retail locations across the United States and stocks a wide range of serving ware, kitchen supplies, and groceries in bulk package sizes.

Smithey Ironware Company

www.smithey.com

Smithey produces beautiful, heavy-duty cookware that functions just as well under the stars and over a campfire as it does in the home kitchen.

APPENDIX C: ADDITIONAL READING AND RESOURCES

Books and Periodicals
Cook's Illustrated and *Cook's Country*
www.cooksillustrated.com and *www.cookscountry.com*

These periodicals from America's Test Kitchen turn common recipes into wonderful re-creations but with less effort. Along the way, the reader learns how and why the recipes work. *Cook's Illustrated* explores fewer dishes but in more detail than *Cook's Country*, its sister publication. These are magazines primarily for the home kitchen, but what you'll learn about indoor cooking will prove invaluable at camp.

Lipsmackin' Camp Cookin'
Christine and Tim Conners, Globe Pequot Press

A recently updated title in the Lipsmackin' series of cookbooks, *Camp Cookin'* covers a wide range of cooking methods and techniques appropriate for the campground setting. Many Dutch oven and skillet recipes are included.

On Food and Cooking: The Science and Lore of the Kitchen
Harold McGee, Scribner

This is an excellent resource for understanding the facts behind cooking. When chefs decipher why recipes work the way they do, they become more effective at adapting recipes in a pinch or creating new ones on the fly. Be forewarned: this is not a cookbook, much less an outdoor cookbook. But if science interests you, this book will too.

The Scout's Campfire Cookbook for Kids
Tim and Christine Conners, Globe Pequot Press

Written with the preteen to young teen audience in mind, the recipes in this book are by no means limited to Scouts. This title has been designed to provide supervising adults with the information they need to give kids safe and appropriate instruction in the unique cooking environment found in outdoor camping. Dutch oven and skillet recipes feature prominently in this book.

The Scout's Dutch Oven Cookbook
Tim and Christine Conners, Globe Pequot Press
Focusing on what is arguably the most popular form of Scout cooking, this book delves into technique without skimping on the recipes. Dozens of Dutch oven experts from throughout Boy Scouts of America contributed over one hundred outstanding and unique camp recipes.

The Scout's Large Groups Cookbook
Tim and Christine Conners, Globe Pequot Press
As with *The Scout's Dutch Oven Cookbook*, Boy Scout leaders spared none of their secrets in providing over one hundred excellent recipes, but in this case with a specific focus on groups of ten to twenty campers or more. A wide range of methods and techniques is covered, many of them centered on cast iron cooking for a crowd.

The Scout's Outdoor Cookbook
Tim and Christine Conners, Globe Pequot Press
The founding title of the Scout's Cookbook series, this book puts more emphasis on the recipes and less on a particular method. All popular forms of camp cooking are represented, but an emphasis is placed on Dutch oven and skillet recipes. Over three hundred recipes are included, many award-winning, and all provided by Scout leaders from across the United States.

Informational Websites
Epicurious
www.epicurious.com
If you're looking to hone your basic cooking skills and could use thousands of recipes for practice, this is a good resource.

Exploratorium
www.exploratorium.edu/cooking
Exploratorium makes cooking fun by putting emphasis on the facts behind it. Even if you're not the scientist type, you'll enjoy this site. Quirky yet practical, recipes flow down the page with relevant explanations posted in the sidebar.

Leave No Trace (LNT)

www.LNT.org

Leave No Trace has been a leader and respected voice in communicating why and how our outdoor places require responsible stewardship. The LNT outdoor ethics code has become standard practice in parks and wild settings throughout the world. More information about the organization is available at their website, and specific information about outdoor ethics principles, especially as applied to cooking, can be found in appendix D of this book.

Lipsmackin' Campin'

www.lipsmackincampin.com

This is Christine and Tim's outdoor cooking website. Here you'll find information about their books as well as numerous helpful articles and instructional videos. Perhaps of most value are links to a large number of professionally produced video tutorials covering a wide range of outdoor cooking-related topics for both camp and trail. These free videos can also be viewed directly on their channel at youtube.com/CampCookingTV.

APPENDIX D: LOW-IMPACT COOKING

Leave No Trace is a widely respected nonprofit organization that communicates and promotes a set of foundational principles for the care of the world's wild places by those who visit them.

These are the seven core principles of Leave No Trace:

- Plan ahead and prepare.

- Travel and camp on durable surfaces.

- Dispose of waste properly.

- Leave what you find.

- Minimize campfire impacts.

- Respect wildlife.

- Be considerate of others.

Careful planning, especially with respect to food preparation, is critical to successfully following the principles of Leave No Trace. When preparing for an upcoming outing, consider the following list of application points as you evaluate your food and cooking options.

Decide how you'll prepare your food.

Some methods of cooking, such as gas stoves and grills, create less impact than others, such as open fires. Low-impact principles are followed when using a camp Dutch oven with charcoal on a fire pan, provided the pan is placed on bare soil or rock, and the coal ash is disposed of in a discreet and fire-safe manner.

When using open fire to cook, follow local fire restrictions and use an established fire ring instead of creating a new one. Keep fires small. If wood gathering is permitted in your camping area, collect wood from the ground rather than from standing trees. To avoid creating barren earth, find wood farther away from camp. Select smaller pieces of wood and burn them completely to ash. Afterward, be sure the fire is completely out. Don't bring firewood from home to camp if the wood might harbor insects or disease harmful to the flora in your camp area.

Carefully select and repackage your food to minimize trash.
Tiny pieces of trash easily become litter. Avoid bringing small, individually packaged candies and other such food items. Twist ties and bread clips are easily lost when dropped. Remove the wrappers and repackage such foods into ziplock bags before leaving home, or use knots instead of ties and clips to seal bags and the like.

Lids from metal cans and broken glass can easily cut or puncture trash sacks. Wrap these carefully before placing them in thin-wall trash bags. Minimize the use of glass in camp. Scan your camp carefully when packing up to ensure that no litter is left behind.

Minimize leftovers and dispose of food waste properly.
Leftover foods make for messier trash and cleanup. If poured on open ground, they are unsightly and unsanitary. If buried, animals may dig them up. Leftovers encourage problem animals to come into camp if not properly managed. Carefully plan your meals to reduce leftovers. And if any remain, share with others or carefully repackage and set aside in a protected place to eat at a later meal.

Dispose of used wash and rinse water (also called gray water) in a manner appropriate for your camping area. Before disposal, remove or strain food chunks from the gray water and place these with the trash. If no dedicated gray water disposal area is available, scatter the water outside of camp in an area free of sensitive vegetation and at least two hundred feet from streams and lakes. Avoid creating too many suds by using only the amount of detergent necessary for the job. Bring only biodegradable soap to camp.

Plan to protect your food, trash, and other odorous items from animals.
Consider avoiding the use of very aromatic foods that can attract animals. Store food, trash, and other odorous items where animals won't be able to get to them. Besides being potentially dangerous to the animal, and inconvenient for the camper, trash is often spread over a large area once the animal gains access. Follow local regulations regarding proper food storage.

Decide whether to avoid collecting wild foods.

Don't harvest wild foods, such as berries, if these are not plentiful in the area you're visiting. Such foods are likely to be a more important component of the local ecosystem when scarce.

These are only a few of the practical considerations and potential applications of the principles of Leave No Trace. Visit www.LNT.org for additional information and ideas.

INDEX

ABOUT THE AUTHORS

Experienced campers, backpackers, and outdoor chefs, Christine and Tim Conners are the authors of the nationally popular Lipsmackin' outdoor cookbook series, including the titles *Lipsmackin' Backpackin'*, *Lipsmackin' Vegetarian Backpackin'*, *Lipsmackin Camp Cookin'*, and their latest entry to the series, *Lipsmackin' Cast Iron Cookin'*.

Specifically for the scouting world, Tim and Christine have produced the Scout's Cookbook series: *The Scout's Outdoor Cookbook*, *The Scout's Dutch Oven Cookbook*, *The Scout's Large Groups Cookbook*, *The Scout's Backpacking Cookbook*, and *The Scout's Campfire Cookbook for Kids*. Each title in the Scout's Cookbook lineup is a collection of unique and outstanding recipes from Scout leaders across the United States.

Christine and Tim have been testing outdoor recipes for nearly thirty years. At the invitation of Boy Scouts of America, they've served several times as judges for *Scouting* magazine's prestigious national camp food cooking contest.

Stop by lipsmackincampin.com to say hello, or check out Christine and Tim's outdoor cooking channel for informative how-to videos at youtube.com/CampCookingTV. Christine's illustrations are used throughout this book. To see more of her work across other mediums, visit artbyconners.com.